Oracle Replication
Expert Methods for Robust Data Sharing

John Garmany
Steve Karam
Donald K. Burleson

RAMPANT TECHPRESS

Oracle Replication
Expert Methods for Robust Data Sharing

By John Garmany, Steve Karam and Donald K. Burleson

Copyright © 2003 by Rampant TechPress. All rights reserved.

Printed in the United States of America.

Published by Rampant TechPress, Kittrell, North Carolina, USA

Oracle In-Focus Series: Book #4

Series Editor: Don Burleson

Editors: Teri Wade

Technical Editor: Robert Freeman

Production Editor: Teri Wade

Cover Design: Janet Burleson

Printing History:

> November 2003 for First Edition

> December 2006 for Second Edition

ISBN 0-9727513-3-5
ISBN-13: 978-0-9727513-3-9

Library of Congress Control Number: 2003097636

Table of Contents

Using the Online Code Depot

Purchase of this book provides complete access to the online code depot that contains the sample scripts. All of the scripts in this book are located at the following URL:

rampant.cc/rep.htm

They will be available for download in a zip format, ready to load and use.

If technical assistance is needed in downloading or accessing the scripts, please contact Rampant TechPress at info@rampant.cc.

Conventions Used in this Book

It is critical for any technical publication to follow rigorous standards and employ consistent punctuation conventions to make the text easy to read.

However, this is not an easy task. Within Oracle there are many types of notation that can confuse a reader. Some Oracle utilities such as STATSPACK and TKPROF are always spelled in CAPITAL letters, while Oracle parameters and procedures have varying naming conventions in the Oracle documentation. It is also important to remember that many Oracle commands are case sensitive, and are always left in their original executable form, and never altered with italics or capitalization.

Hence, all Rampant TechPress books follow these conventions:

- **Parameters** - All Oracle parameters will be *lowercase italics*. Exceptions to this rule are parameter arguments that are commonly capitalized (KEEP pool, TKPROF), these will be left in ALL CAPS.

- **Variables** – All PL/SQL program variables and arguments will also remain in lowercase italics (*dbms_job, dbms_utility*).

- **Tables & dictionary objects** – All data dictionary objects are referenced in lowercase italics (*dba_indexes, v$sql*). This includes all *v$* and *x$* views (*x$kcbcbh, v$parameter*) and dictionary views (*dba_tables, user_indexes*).

- **SQL** – All SQL is formatted for easy use in the code depot, and all SQL is displayed in lowercase. The main SQL terms (select, from, where, group by, order by, having) will always appear on a separate line.

- **Programs & Products** – All products and programs that are known to the author are capitalized according to the vendor specifications (IBM, DBXray, etc). All names known by Rampant TechPress to be trademark names appear in this text as initial caps. References to UNIX are always made in uppercase.

Preface

Replication has a fearsome reputation as the most difficult Oracle function to create and maintain. One reason for this trepidation is the level of complexity and the overwhelming documentation. But replication need not be so inaccessible. The first goal of the book is to explain how and why replication exists and to provide a solid basis for planning and implementing a replication environment.

The second goal is to be as complete as possible within the constraints of the book. A book is never more frustrating than when it directs a reader to do something and does not provide instruction on how to do it. These authors have tried not to assume anything and provide as much explanation as possible.

Finally, this book is not the whole story of replication. The Oracle documentation is thousands of pages long. With the advent of Oracle Streams, new methods of replication are being introduced. This book is a first stop. Hopefully, this book provides the tools needed to take the leap into Oracle Replication.

A Survey of Oracle Replication

Oracle replication has been around for quite some time and has become a mature, feature-rich environment to satisfy widely dispersed processing requirements. Replication was first introduced as a way to allow Oracle tables or subsets of tables to be available locally on widely separated database servers. This was accomplished via the use of snapshots, or point-in-time copies, of required tables that were copied from a master server to one or more remote slave servers. The snapshot technique was particularly effective for relatively static tables that did not require frequent refresh operations to be kept in sync with the master tables. Read-only applications benefited from the use of snapshots since wide-area network transmission time was eliminated which significantly improved performance.

Snapshots are now more commonly known as materialized views, and while the creation of remote materialized views of master tables is still a common use of replication, the technology has matured significantly, supporting a much broader spectrum of database objects. The snapshot method will be introduced followed by more advanced techniques.

A number of factors influence the decisions concerning Oracle table replication. As shown in the graph below, table size and the volatility of the table data are of particular importance. Smaller static tables are ideal candidates for snapshot replication for remote read-only applications, whereas larger, dynamic master tables with many inserts, updates, and deletes would require frequent refreshes consuming a large amount of system and network resources. Snapshots are not a good solution for these large, dynamic master tables, so more advanced techniques should be used.

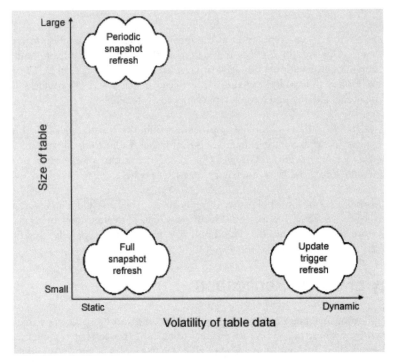

Figure P.1: *Volatility vs. Table Size*

When considering system and network performance, the DBA needs to be concerned with the size of the snapshots created and the frequency they are created or refreshed. As indicated in the figure above, a snapshot can be re-created or a full refresh can be performed whenever required. Periodic refreshes can be scheduled or a trigger can be used to refresh changes from a master table to the slave snapshots. Use the following general rules to determine which methodology is most appropriate.

Small static table replication

When a table is small and contains relatively static data, it is often simpler to drop and then re-create the snapshot than it is to use the REFRESH COMPLETE option. A simple script invoked via *cron* could be created to perform the drop and re-creation at predetermined intervals.

An alternative to creating a snapshot is to use distributed SQL to create the replicated table directly on the slave database. Notice how a database link is utilized in the following CTAS example to create a subset of the master *emp* table from the headquarters database:

```
CREATE TABLE emp_nc
AS SELECT
    emp_nbr,
    emp_name,
    emp_phone,
    emp_hire_date
FROM
    emp@hq
WHERE
    department = 'NC';
```

Small dynamic table replication

For small tables, an update trigger could be invoked to perform a refresh. However, since the table is small, the snapshot log would probably not contain very many changes. It is therefore entirely feasible that propagating the changes to the snapshot at more frequent intervals would be a suitable solution. Here is an example of a REFRESH FAST specification that propagates every hour:

```
CREATE SNAPSHOT
    cust_snap1
REFRESH FAST
    START WITH SYSDATE
    NEXT SYSDATE + 1/24
AS
SELECT
    cust_nbr, cust_name
FROM
    customer@hq
WHERE
    department = 'NC';
```

Large static table replication

For larger tables with static data content, the refresh interval can be significantly increased. The following example performs a REFRESH COMPLETE on the first Sunday of each quarter:

```
CREATE SNAPSHOT
    cust_snap1
REFRESH COMPLETE
    START WITH SYSDATE
    NEXT NEXT_DAY(ADD_MONTHS(trunc(sysdate,'Q'),3),'SUNDAY')
AS
SELECT
    cust_nbr, cust_name
FROM
    customer@hq
WHERE
    department = 'NC';
```

Large dynamic table replication

Dropping and re-creating very large tables is not a good option because of the system and network resources consumed. The same holds true for using the REFRESH COMPLETE option; both options would take too much time. There are better options to use for these tables.

An Overview of Multimaster replication

Oracle now supports multiple master tables as a feature of advanced replication. Modifications to any of the master tables from any of the sites are propagated to other masters either synchronously or asynchronously. Oracle's advanced replication feature, using multimaster replication and synchronous updates, is probably a good choice for the replication of large, dynamic tables that can be updated from multiple locations. Using this technology, table updates are propagated as they occur, eliminating the need to refresh snapshots across the network.

Implementing multimaster replication significantly improves end-user response time where databases that require updating by users from diverse locations are involved. Additionally, multimaster replication provides load balancing and recovery fail-over solutions.

Oracle's multimaster replication utilizes peer-to-peer replication techniques to synchronize all of the master tables in the network, regardless of where they are. Changes to a table at any master site are propagated to other master sites either synchronously or asynchronously.

The benefits do not come without a price. Configuring multimaster replication is a sophisticated process. Complexity is compounded by the need to implement conflict resolution processes, especially in the case of asynchronous propagation of changes. Larger installations could spend hundreds of hours configuring replication and may require a dedicated DBA to manage the environment. Regardless, most installations find that the benefits are well worth the extra effort.

In addition to the table replication capabilities of multimaster replication, which is far superior to read-only snapshot replication, the replication of additional database objects is supported, including:

- Indexes
- Index types
- Packages / Package Bodies
- Procedures / Functions

- Synonyms

- Tables

- Triggers

- User-Defined Operators, Types, and Type Bodies

- Views and Object Views

The ability to replicate stored procedures, for instance, allows the DBA to roll out code changes as easily as table data changes. This is particularly useful in shops where all application code is encapsulated within stored procedures.

Multimaster replication can be thought of as a synchronized set of updatable snapshots. In this context, *updatable* means that the snapshot allows the FOR UPDATE clause within its definition. In the example below, the snapshot propagates its updates back to the master table:

```
create snapshot
   customer_updatable_snap
refresh fast start with sysdate
next sysdate + 1/24
for update
query rewrite
  as
    select * from customer@master_site;
```

Conclusion

This preface has laid the foundation for the more complex material to follow and the complex details of Oracle replication will now be explored.

Oracle Replication Architecture

What is Replication?

Database Replication is the copying of part or all of a database to a remote site. The remote site may be in another part of the world, or right next to the primary site.

Many people believe that replication is no longer necessary because of the reliability and speed of the Internet. It is true that distributed transactions provide access to real-time data almost anywhere in the world, but they require that all databases operate all the time. When one database is down for any reason, other databases can no longer access its data. Replication solves this problem because each site has a copy of the data.

Replication of all or part of a database is becoming more common for all sorts of reasons. Replication can be used to feed data into a data warehouse, or relieve a primary database from the workload of producing reports. It can be used to load-balance users. However, heavy updating can cause the overhead of replication to outweigh the benefit of multiple systems.

Replication can be used in high-availability databases that require zero-failover using Transparent Application Failover (TAF). Replication is commonly utilized to create a database that contains a subset of the master database for security purposes. Also, replication can be used to improve performance, as querying local data is generally faster than querying the same data over a network link. Database replication does have limitations, and understanding those limitations can insure the success of a replication project.

This chapter is an introduction to Oracle replication. First, manual replication techniques will be reviewed, followed by a quick tour of the Oracle replication architecture. Then other Oracle replication offerings will be explored, such as basic and advanced replication. Finally, some potential answers will be presented the question of which type of replication is right for a given situation.

Manual Replication Techniques

The simplest form of replication just creates a copy of a table on another database. This can be done using the Oracle exp/imp utilities, create table as select (CTAS), or transportable tablespaces.

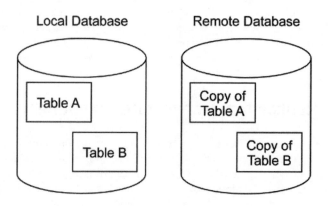

Figure 1.1: *Replication of Table A and Table B*

The advantages of this form of replication are that the databases are not continuously exchanging data. Setup and maintenance are easy, and errors that are discovered during the move and can be corrected on the spot. The drawbacks of this type of replication are that there is no way to keep data current or propagate changes made to the base tables.

Another way of replicating data is via Oracle's Data Guard. Data Guard allows the creation of exact copies of a database and the replication of changes on the primary database to the Physical Standby in real time. Data Guard is fairly easy to setup and to use, but it is not as flexible as replication is in many ways, so it may or may not be the right solution. The Physical Standby database is left in "recovery" mode. As archivelogs are created on the primary they are applied to the standby. The standby can be opened in read-only mode but changes are not applied until the standby is returned to recovery mode. The longer it is open, the farther behind the primary it falls. One useful form of Data Guard is a Logical Standby. The Logical Standby uses SQL Apply to add changes from the primary database to the standby database. The Logical Standby can be open and in use while changes are being applied. The

Logical Standby may be an acceptable choice if only part of the primary database is needed for activities like adding objects to the database such as materialized views or indexes to support reporting.

Replication can also be facilitated in the form of PL/SQL packages and database triggers. The DBA can create a trigger that captures a row modification on a table, and forwards that change to a remote table. If both tables implement the trigger, changes are propagated back and forth, keeping both tables in sync.

This is more difficult than it may first appear because the procedures must ensure that the trigger does not forward an update being propagated from another database, and they must implement some sort of primary key collision resolution. If this kind of replication is needed, there is no need to reinvent the wheel. Instead, this book will explore the magic of Oracle replication.

The Oracle Replication Architecture Components

The replication overview will start with an examination of the different architectural components that come into play. This section will first look at the principle objects used in replication: table, materialized views, and materialized view logs. Next, the two different types of replication, basic and advanced, will be reviewed. The final topic will be the job scheduler, which provides the ability to schedule replicated jobs.

Tables and Replication

Replication begins with one or more tables. Tables, of course, store the data that is to be replicated to other databases. In replication parlance, a table is known as the target master, or the target or source of the replication. A materialized view, which will be examined in the next section, can also be a target master. Tables with LONG or LONG RAW data types cannot be replicated. Consider LOB datatypes instead, CLOB and BLOB for example, when creating tables so that the design will allow replication to be implemented later.

Here is an example of the creation of a table:

```
Create table parts
(     part_number         number primary key,
      part_description    varchar2(30),
      bin_location        varchar2(5),
      cost                number,
      list                number,
      fleet               number,
      on_hand             number)
tablespace parts_data;
```

Materialized Views

The principle object in a simple replication environment is the materialized view. A *materialized view* (MView) is an Oracle object that is much like a regular table in that it stores data. The data stored in an MView is derived from the results of an SQL query associated with the materialized view. A materialized view has a number of uses, but this section explores its use as a means to create a replicated environment.

Here is an example of the creation of an Mview:

```
Create or replace materialized view mv_parts
As
Select * from parts@parts_db;
```

When created for replication, materialized views will be assigned a number of different attributes that define things such as refresh schedules and refresh methods, which will be discussed later in this chapter. A read-only Mview on a subset of rows or columns can also be created, as seen in this example:

```
Create or replace materialized view mv_parts
As
Select part_number, part_description, on_hand
from parts@parts_db
where bin_location='OKC';
```

In this case, an Mview was created that only displays the part number, description, and the on hand quantity for all parts with BIN_LOCATION equal to the value of OKC. This allows the data that is available to other systems that might be using the Mview to be restricted.

Materialized View Logs

Some methods of replication involve the application of only the changes that apply to a given Mview. This is known as a *fast refresh*. Fast refreshes are made possible, in part, through the use of the *Materialized View Log* (Mview Log). The Mview log tracks all the changes that occur in the object that the Mview log is assigned. Those changes (or deltas) are then applied to the remote Mviews. Here is an example of the creation of an Mview log:

```
Create materialized view log on table parts;
```

Database links

Like distributed transactions, all types of replication require database links to communicate between databases. The easiest way to think of a database link is to

---

view it as one database establishing an SQLPLUS session with another database. The initiating database acts like a client and sends a request to the remote database. The remote database executes the request and returns the results. Database links use Oracle Net name resolution services such as *tnsnames.ora*, Names or LDAP server to resolve the remote database connection in the same way SQLPLUS does.

If a *tnsnames.ora* file is being used, the database will only use the *tnsnames.ora* file located in the $ORACLE_HOME/network/admin directory, or the location pointed to by the *tns_admin* environment parameter setting. Also, if the link is going to require the use of a domain name server, then global names must be used, with *global_names* = true. Each database in the replication must have a unique global name.

Creating a database link is quite easy. Here is an example of the creation of a database link called *parts* to a database called *partsdb*. When this database link is accessed, it will log onto the remote database as the user "admin," using the password "administrator"

```
create public database link parts_link
    connect to admin identified by administrator
    using 'partsdb';
```

Note that it is important that the service name *partsdb* resolve to an actual database. Thus, *partsdb* must exist in either the *tnsnames.ora*, the name server, or whatever name-resolution service being used.

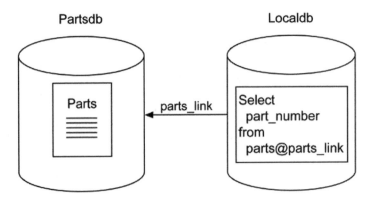

Figure 1.2: *Connecting with a Database Link*

The link that was just created need to be tested. Here is some sample SQL that does just that:

```
select
   part_number
from
   parts@parts_link;
```

In this example, a table called *parts* is being accessed. However, the query is not being executed against a table called *parts* on the current database. Instead, the *user_tables* being queried exists on a database that is pointed to by the service name *parts_link*, as denoted by the syntax "@parts_link."

🖥 User ID = book, password = reader

Also, note something else about this query. Remember, when the *parts_link* database link was created, it was defined to connect to the admin schema. If the table *parts* was not in the admin schema, an error would be generated after issuing this query indicating that the table does not exist. The moral of this story is that even with database links, security rules still apply. The admin schema will either need to own the *parts* table, or it will need a grant to the *parts* table if it should lie in another schema. The following is an example of a query against the *parts* table in the *parts_link* database, and this time the *parts* table is in a schema called *parts_schema* rather than admin:

```
select
   part_number
from
   parts_schema.parts@parts_link;
```

Of course, read permission will need to be granted to admin on *parts_schema.parts* in order for this query to work. Another alternative to prefixing the object name with the schema name is to use synonyms, private or public, but private is preferred.

If the link is going to require the use of a domain name server, then global names must be used, with *global_names* = TRUE. Each database in the replication must have a unique global name. When creating read-only or updatable materialized views, the only required link is from the remote site to the master site with the base tables. Since the remote site initiates both the data push and pull, there is no need for a link from the master site back to the remote site. For multi-master replication, links must be established between both master sites.

Refresh Groups

Sometimes Mviews need to be consistent with each other. This requires that they be refreshed together. To accomplish this, Mviews can be assigned to refresh groups.

When the Mviews are refreshed in a refresh group, all of the Mviews in that group will be refreshed to the same consistent point and time.

Refresh Methods

If they are not refreshed, the data in an Mview will become stale and will not reflect the data as it looks in the target table. Oracle offers several different methods of refreshing the Mview:

- **Fast Refresh** – This causes the Mview to be updated with only the rows that have changed since it was last refreshed. An Mview Log on the target table must exist in order to be able to fast refresh a view in Oracle. Fast refreshes have the benefit of not taking much time.

- **Complete Refresh** – A complete refresh will cause the entire Mview to be truncated and then repopulated by data from the master table. This can be a very expensive operation in terms of both resources and time.

- **Force Refresh** – This refresh method will cause Oracle to refresh using a fast refresh, if that is possible. If a fast refresh is not possible, Oracle will perform a complete refresh. This refresh method helps eliminate problems in certain cases where the Mview fast refresh would fail.

Types of Oracle Replication

The next section will introduce the different forms of Oracle replication. There are two principle types of replication within Oracle:

- Basic Replication
- Advanced Replication

Basic Replication

Basic replication provides an elementary means to replicate data between databases. Basic replication is always one-way. In basic replication, the table that is being replicated is called the *target master table* or the target Mview, in the case of an Mview. The database that this table belongs in is known as the *master definition site*. On the master definition site, an Mview log might be created to allow for fast refreshes.

Once the table is created at the master definition site, optionally with an Mview log, read-only Mviews can be created at each *destination site*. These read-only materialized views will refresh against the master table on the master definition site through a dblink. Once the Mview is created at each destination site, data will flow one way; from the table on the master definition site to each Mview on the destination site.

The data movement is controlled on the destination site via the job scheduler, which is a topic covered later in this Chapter.

Advanced Replication

Advanced replication is only available with the Enterprise edition of Oracle, though updateable and Writeable Mviews are available in the Standard edition. It provides more complex replication solutions such as:

- Updateable Materialized Views

- Writeable Materialized Views

- Multi-Master replication

- Procedural replication

Updateable Materialized Views

Basic replication also allows for updateable Mviews. Use *Updateable Mviews* if there is a need to perform insert, update, or delete operations on the destination site Mviews. Once the destination site is updated, those updates will replicate to any other sites that may be configured. Thus, replication becomes two-way between the destination site and the master site. In order to support updatable Mviews, a replicaton group must be set up and the updatabale Mviews should be assigned to that replication group.

Writeable Materialized Views

Oracle also allows Writeable Materialized Views. Writeable Materialized Views allow users to perform DML operations on the Mview. However, none of the changes to the Mview will be replicated to the target table. Also, these changes will be lost the next time the view refreshes.

Multi-Master Replication

Multi-master replication provides support for simultaneous updates of other master tables that exist at multiple sites. Rather than there being just one master site, as with basic replication, multi-master replication supports multiple master sites. Each master site communicates changes to the other master sites. Thus, simultaneous changes to the same record at each master site are supported. Conflicts in the changes are resolved through a set of rules. Advanced replication does not use Mviews as in the other forms of replication, but rather uses a generated trigger and two stored packages.

Building an advanced replication system consists of several steps. Most of these steps are completed with a stored procedure, which is listed:

1. A master replication group is defined (*dbms_repcat.create_master_repgrp*).

2. Each master definition site is defined. The master definition site contains the tables that will be replicated. (*dbms_repcat.add_master_database*).

3. Objects to be replicated are placed in a replication group (*dbms_repcat.create_master_repobject*)

4. Each object has replication support added (*dbms_repcat.generate_replication_support*). Replication support consists of all the internal triggers and support tables needed to track changes.

5. Now, start replication via the *dbms_repcat.resume_master_activity* stored procedure.

More details on implementing advanced replication, along with examples, can be found in Chapter 4, *Updatable Materialized Views*, and Chapter 6, *Multi-Master Replication.*

So, how does replication actually happen with Multi-master replication? Once replication is established, propagation of changes among the remote or master sites is the job of the *deferred transaction queue*. All changes are placed in the deferred transaction queue, which sends those changes across a database link to the deferred transaction queue on the remote master site.

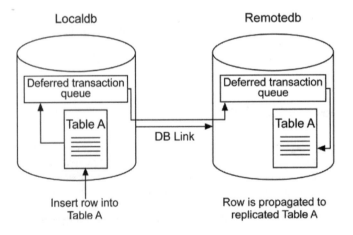

Figure 1.3: *Replication using the Deferred Transaction Queue*

The remote master site then applies those changes to the objects in its replication group. This form of propagation continues until all sites have received the change. If the change cannot be pushed to the remote site because of network problems or the database is down, the change is removed from the deferred transaction queue and placed in the local deferred error queue.

If the change is pushed to the remote site but cannot be applied to the replication object, it is placed in the remote site's deferred error queue. Once a change has been placed in the deferred error queue, no changes can be pushed from the deferred transaction queue. In other words, replication stops until the change in the deferred error queue is either fixed and applied, or deleted from the queue. This, of course, is the job of the DBA. More detail on error correction will be provided in Chapter 7.

Multi-master replication can be synchronous or asynchronous. Asynchronous is the default. Care should be taken with either method. When using synchronous replication, the failure of any replicated site can cause the database to come to a screeching halt. There is also a possibility of losing data when using asynchronous replication.

Procedural Replication

Procedural replication allows a procedure to be called at each remote site with the same arguments. Each site will have a copy of the same procedure, as does the master site. The procedure is first executed at the master site. Then, using the *dbms_defer_sys.execute* package at the master site, the same procedure can be executed at each of the remote sites.

Why use procedural replication? Since normal replication works on a row level, larger bulk operations can be cumbersome to replicate because of the load on the network. Procedural replication allows procedures to be called that can perform operations such as bulk deletes on a table or massive data changes. Procedural replication will not replicate the modifications that are made by the procedure, but the table can continue to be replicated.

Streams Replication will be covered in more detail later in this book. Streams Replication was introduced in Oracle9i and is a low impact method of implementing one or n-way replication. Basically Streams Replication has three components: a capture process, a propagator, and an apply process. The capture process uses Log Miner to extract changes from the online or archive redo logs. The propagator sends the changes to the remote database across a dblink and the apply process applies the changes to the remote database. Streams Replication uses the SQL Apply method, similar to a Logical Standby. Because the capture process is extracting changes from the redo logs, there is no impact on the database processes. The apply process is just another server process applying changes. While these extra processes are overhead to the server, they have a minimal impact compared to Advanced Replication.

Streams Replication replicates in one direction. To get data replicating in both directions, Streams would need to be implemented on the remote site, back to the local site. The result is Streams Replication going in both directions.

Which Form of Replication is Right for You?

Determining which type of replication the particular situation requires is very important. Remember: these two adages:

- More is NOT always better!

- Just because Oracle includes it in the database doesn't mean it has to be used!

One of the biggest mistakes a company can make is to implement advanced replication when all that is needed is read-only materialized views. With replication, "more" is harder to implement, harder to maintain, harder to troubleshoot, and takes more time.

Here are some questions to ask to determine the level of replication that best fits the situation.

- Is the transfer of data time sensitive?

   Many DBAs believe that data is time sensitive when in fact it is not. If the data is being moved to a data warehouse to be used for data mining or report generation, the data is probably not time sensitive. A daily or even weekly transfer may meet the entire business requirement. Ask management. A daily report in the morning may be acceptable instead of a report available on demand with the most recent data. Many DBAs are finding that even internal materialized views are taking so long to update that they have to update them at night or only on weekends.

- Is the number of tables manageable?

   If Oracle Applications is being used, forget about replicating the entire database. Oracle Apps consist of tens of thousands of tables. This scenario is not a candidate for replication. However, replicating parts of large databases is possible. Remember that each replicated object adds overhead to the databases and takes network bandwidth. There are practical limits to the number of objects can be replicated, depending on the capability of the database server and the network connections. Replicating 100 tables is easy, a thousand may not be possible, ten thousand - forget it.

- Do all replicated tables need to be updatable?

   This is a big one. A shop will often set up full multi-master replication because the database is supporting an application that has to update certain tables. Tables that need to be updated at both locations must use advanced replication, however all remaining tables can use basic replication. This ability to mix replication types can significantly lower the replication overhead. Remember, less is best.

- Does the database change constantly?

  Does QA roll in a new update every weekend? If so, replication may not be feasible. Table changes may force the rebuild of replication or implementation of advanced replication. Maintaining replication in a changing database will entail a significant increase in the DBA's workload. In later chapters, the methods of implementing changes in the objects being replicated will be covered.

- Is the number of transactions manageable?

  The number of transactions per minute is another one of those variables that must be considered. A replication based on a few tables will be better able to handle high numbers of transactions. A large replication may not be able to keep up on a high transaction system, and this again depends on the server capabilities and the network bandwidth.

- Is replication occurring between different versions of Oracle or different operating systems?

  Many shops choose replication rather than a standby database precisely because replication can operate between either different versions of the Oracle database, or between Oracle databases running on different operating systems. Because replication is passed across database links, different versions of Oracle can be used. An Oracle database on Windows can be replicated to a database on a Sun Server, thereby providing a failover solution if needed.

- Do both sites require the ability to update the same tables?

  If both sides of the replication must update data, then advanced replication must be implemented. Use advanced replication only on the tables that must be updated on both sides of the replication.

- Does the replicated site require the ability to replicate to another site?

  A master site can replicate with other sites. If the remote site only replicates with one master site, use updateable materialized views. If the remote site must replicate the data further, then it too must be a master site and multi-master replication is required.

Conclusion

It may seem that replication is difficult to understand and time-consuming to setup. But its daunting reputation is much worse than the reality. Once it is set up and operating, it really isn't very intimidating. Remember to replicate at the lowest level possible. Don't use advanced replication where basic replication will work. Don't try to replicate more objects than the server and network are able to support.

The remainder of this book focuses on implementing replication by example. Chapter 2 will cover installing replication support in the database. Each type of replication is explored in a self-contained chapter. So, it is possible to jump straight to the chapter on multi-master replication. However, it's not recommended.

Preparing to Use
Oracle Replication

CHAPTER

2

This chapter covers the setup that is required for basic replication as well as advanced replication. The additional setup requirements for advanced replication will also be examined. The chapter will wrap up with a review of the replication packages that Oracle provides.

Determining which Replication Method is right for you

Early on, it will be necessary to decide between master site replication and materialized view replication. Here are the benefits of each of these types of replication.

First, materialized view replication offers these features:

- Simplified replication configuration.

- The ability to control what is replicated from the master site.

- The ability to replicate in both directions.

- The ability to replicate from a remote table or a remote materialized view.

- Read-only snapshots are available with all editions of Oracle.

In comparison, replicated sites offer the following benefits:

- Support for more complex forms of replication, including multi-master replication.

- Provides support for high availability architectures.

- Provides superior support for DML operations

- DML changes are allowed without locking tables.

Consider these advantages when selecting your method of replication.

> 🔔 Prior to Oracle8i, materialized views were known as snapshots. Throughout this book, the expressions can be used interchangeably, but materialized view is most common.

Common Replication Setup

Both basic and advanced replication have some common setup requirements. In this section, these requirements will be covered. They include the following:

- Configuring database parameters
- Configuring replication user accounts
- Configuring database links
- Configuring objects for replication
- Other replication configuration issues

The following section explores these configuration items in a bit more detail.

Configuring Database Parameters

Several database parameters should be set for replication including:

PARAMETER NAME	DEFAULT VALUE	RECOMMENDED VALUE
compatible	Depends on the version of Oracle being used.	Set compatible to the version of Oracle that is being used in order to access all replication features of that version of the database
global_names	FALSE	It is required to set global_names to TRUE in each database that will be involved in advanced replication.
job_queue_ processes	0	This parameter must be set to a value of at least one. Higher values will allow more parallel replication of objects.
open_links	4	open_links defines the number of concurrent database links that are required for a given database. This parameter needs to be configured for 1 additional link for each database that will be replicated to. So, if 6 databases will be replicating, this value should be set to 6.

PARAMETER NAME	DEFAULT VALUE	RECOMMENDED VALUE
parallel_automatic_ tuning	FALSE	Oracle9i offers this parameter to help establish the correct level of parallelism. Set to TRUE to allow Oracle to determine the best configuration for parallel operations.
parallel_max_ servers	Derived based on the parameters: cpu_count, parallel_automatic_ tuning, parallel_ adaptive_multi_user	This is only important for parallel propagation, which is recommended. Configure this parameter's value high enough to allow sufficient parallel servers to be started. Generally, the default is sufficient.
parallel_min_ servers	0	Set this value to the number of parallel streams is expected.
processes	Derived from the value of the parameter parallel_max_ servers	Should be set high enough to allow all Oracle-related processes to operate.
replication_ dependency_ tracking	TRUE	Should be set to the default value.
shared_pool_size	OS Dependent	Will usually need to be increased for replication environments. Generally, adding 20m for basic replication and 40m for advanced replication is sufficient.

Configuring the Replication User Accounts

Typically, when creating a replication environment specific schemas will be created for the replication operations. Basic replication requires two schemas, whereas advanced replication requires additional schemas. The following section provides more detail.

Basic Replication Schemas

The first schema to create is the *repadmin* schema. This is the schema that will own any objects that will be replicated, including multi-master environments. The *repadmin* schema will also own the schedules for propagation of the replicated objects that will be created.

Here is an example of the creation of the REPADMIN user:

```
CREATE USER repadmin IDENTIFIED BY repadmin
DEFAULT TABLESPACE replicated_data
TEMPORARY TABLESPACE temp;
```

The create materialized view system privilege will be granted to the *repadmin* schema, as seen here:

```
GRANT CREATE MATERIALIZED VIEW TO repadmin;
```

On any target database that a database link will be connecting, a user called REPUSER will be created. All database links will be created to the REPUSER database account. Here is an example of the creation of the REPUSER user:

```
CREATE USER repuser IDENTIFIED BY repuser
DEFAULT TABLESPACE replicated_data
TEMPORARY TABLESPACE temp;
```

If the objects being replicated are not owned by REPUSER, access will need to be granted to objects that will be replicated if they exist in schemas other than *repuser*. This is done with the GRANT command. The GRANT will need to be issued either as the owner of the object, or if using Oracle9i and later, the GRANT can be issued as SYS. Here is an example of the use of the GRANT command to grant select privileges to the *repuser* schema on the table called *my_tab*, which is owned by the *tab_own* schema:

```
GRANT SELECT ON tab_own.my_tab TO repuser;
```

Private synonyms can also be created for the objects that are going to be replicated using the create synonym command as seen in this example:

```
CREATE SYNONYM my_tab FOR tab_own.my_tab;
```

Advanced Replication Schemas

Advanced Replication requires the creation of the following schemas:

- Repproxy
- Repadmin

These schemas implement a number of replication related functions:

- The proxy schema at the master site provides limited access to the objects in the master replication group.

- Receivers on the master site get the transactions pushed by the propagators and apply them to objects on the master site.

- The replication administrator is on the remote site and is responsible for creating and maintaining the materialized view groups.

- The *repadmin* schema is also the schema in which the propagators push transactions to the receiver on the master site.

- Refreshers on the remote site run from the *repadmin* schema and pull changes from the master site objects. They then apply the changes to the remote site objects.

The master site schema *repproxy* executes the actual replication communication from the remote site. *Repproxy* is the master site proxy and receiver. It also provides changes to the refresher.

On the remote site, replication is administered by *repadmin*. *Repadmin* is the snapshot administrator, the propagator, and the refresher. A database link connects *repadmin* with *repproxy*. Using a private link restricts user access to the base tables on the master site. *Repproxy* is granted rights to the objects being replicated. *Repadmin* on the remote site contacts *repproxy* and pushes changes, which *repproxy* applies. *Repadmin* then pulls changed data from *repproxy* to update the remote site.

Security requirements for the *repadmin* and *repproxy* schemas will be covered in later chapters. Database links will be covered in the next section.

Configuring Database links for Basic Replication

After creating the *repadmin* schema, the database links need to be created that allow the replication environment to be created. The following section explores what a database link is and when they are required for replication. After that, the reader will be ready to create some database links.

Database Links

If any form of replication is being used, database links will need to be configured. Database links are the communication channels used by the databases for distributed database activities. Database links are one-way connections, and each link connects a database to one, and only one, other database. For example, database *db1* can use a link to connect to database *db2*. Across that link, database *db1* queries or sends updates to objects in database *db2*.

The database link created on database *db1* is a one-way communication link between database *db1* to database *db2*. A separate database link would need to be created from database *db2* to database *db1*, in order to allow database *db2* to act on objects in database *db1*.

In the case of basic replication, only the database with the table being replicated needs to have a database link created. Advanced replication, however, requires database links on all databases involved in the replication operations.

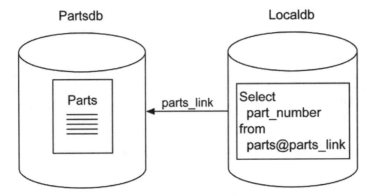

Figure 2.1: *Database Links*

The next section covers creating Oracle database links.

Creating Database Links

Database links are critical to the successful operation of replication, and it's important to have a thorough understanding of how they work and how they are created. The following section covers in more detail the basics of creating links, and then provides some details that are specific to creating links with advanced replication.

Creating Database Links – The Basics

Database links are created via the CREATE DATABASE LINK command. By default, database links are private, which means they are only accessible through the schema in which they are created. Here is an example of the creation of a private database link:

```
CONNECT scott/tiger
CREATE DATABASE LINK paris
   CONNECT TO admin IDENTIFIED BY administrator
   USING 'parisdb';
```

Note that only those in the *scott* schema can access the database link created above. But often, it will be necessary for all database schemas to be able to access the database link. In that case, use the PUBLIC clause of the CREATE DATABASE LINK command as seen in this example:

```
CREATE PUBLIC DATABASE LINK paris
    CONNECT TO admin IDENTIFIED BY administrator
    USING 'parisdb';
```

Both the java based OEM and the web based DBConsole have the ability to visually create DBLinks. With Oracle 10g, the Java based OEM will need to be installed to support replication because all the features are not yet implemented in the web based DBConsole. In 10g, OEM is relegated to the Client install and is no longer installed with the database. In 9i, OEM is installed with the database install.

DBAs that use Oracle Enterprise Manager can use the GUI to create database links as well. The following graphics provide an example of the creation of a database link via OEM:

1. Open Oracle Enterprise Manager and select the user (schema) that will use the link.

2. Right click on the user's name and select create. OEM will present the Create Menu (Figure 2.2).

Figure 2.2: *Oracle Enterprise Manager Create Menu*

3. Select **Database Link** and **Create**. OEM will present the Create Database Link window as shown in Figure 2.3.

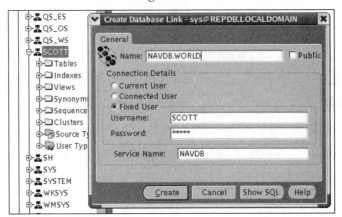

Figure 2.3: *Oracle Enterprise Manager Create Database Link*

4. Enter the name of the link. Remember, if Global Names is being used, the link name must match the Global Name of the database being linked to. In Figure 2.3, the link is connecting to *navdb.world*. For security, it is connecting to the SCOTT user. The service name in the local *tnsnames.ora* file for *navdb.world* is called NAVDB.

5. OEM displays database links under the Distributed Tab. Expanding the SCOTT user and selecting the *navdb.world* link will display the information about the link (Figure 2.4). Notice that all fields except the TEST button are grayed out. This is because you cannot modify a database link. If changes are required, delete the link and recreate it with the updated information.

Figure 2.4: *Oracle Enterprise Manager Database Link Information*

6. To test the link, simply select the Test button. If the connection defined by the link is successful, OEM will report that the link is active, as shown in Figure 2.5. If it was not successful, OEM simply reports that the link is inactive.

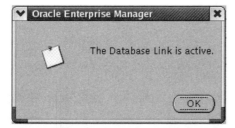

Figure 2.5: *Oracle Enterprise Manager Database Link Status*

There are a few other items of interest. First, database links are normally opened on first use and remain open, even if not used again, until the user session ends. In replication, the link is open on first use and remains open. Since job processes perform replication, the session never actually closes. If the link does get closed, as in a network failure for instance, it will be reopened on the next use.

Creating Database Links – Setup Your Replication Environment

When setting up a basic replication environment, the REPADMIN user is created first. Once the REPADMIN user is created, the next step is to create the database links. These links allow replication of the source data to the remote database, and vice-versa if advanced replication is being used.

With advanced replication, a number of database links may be needed. Only private database links can be used with advanced replication, though public database links can come in handy. A public link can be established and then a private link can be placed on the public link. This allows the removal of the USING clause in every private db link that is created.

Here is an example. First, create a public link to the remote database without providing a log on. Second, use that public link to create a private link for the replication.

After connecting as SYSTEM, create the public link.

```
CREATE PUBLIC DATABASE LINK paris.my_domain USING 'parisdb';
```

The public link to the *parisdb* database is created without a login. Note that the remote database's global name is being used.

Next, the link that the administrator will use to connect to the remote database is created. Recall that the local administrator is REPADMIN and the remote administrator is REPPROXY. Now, log into REPADMIN and create the private database link.

```
CREATE DATABASE LINK paris.my_domain
  CONNECT TO snapproxy IDENTIFIED by sn_passwd;
```

Notice that the private link has the same name as the public link. Actually, the private link rides on the public link. For this reason, the using clause is not needed. It doesn't have to be done this way. If the DBA prefers, several private database links could be created.

Now it's time to consider the objects used in replication.

Configuring Objects for Replication

If the plan is to use basic replication, then carefully consider the following when designing the objects to be replicated:

- Make sure the table has a primary key. If a primary key can't be created, then there must be a set of columns in the table that makes each row unique. While basic replication allows replication of a table based on ROWID, advanced forms of replication require some method of identifying rows in the table via a primary key.

- Replication supports almost every column type available in Oracle, including user-defined datatypes. However, the following objects are not supported by replication:

  - LONG

  - LONG RAW

  - BFILE

  - UROWID

Other Configuration Issues

To say that replication is system-intensive can be an understatement. There are a number of ancillary database administrative issues to be considered when using replication.

The first is the issue of rollback segment space. Replication of large objects, particularly the initial creation of replicated objects or full refreshes of existing objects, can use an inordinate amount of rollback/undo segment space. Thus, make the rollback segments or UNDO tablespace larger if using automated undo. If using manual rollback segments, carefully watch their usage patterns and make sure they are configured properly. It is highly recommended that automatic UNDO management be used.

When adding replicated objects to a database, space utilization grows as well. This must be carefully managed to avoid failed replication. Carefully calculate the space requirements of the tablespaces. Add space if required and unless there is a compelling reason not to, set the tablespaces to autoextend.

Finally, Oracle networking needs to be working between each of the databases. Oracle Net should be configured in order to be able to replicate between databases.

Overview of Replication Packages

Basic replication is simply a materialized view built across a database link. There is no need to install replication packages in order to use basic replication. However, all advanced replication methods require the replication catalog and packages be installed. With Oracle9i and above, the replication catalog and associated package are installed automatically. Earlier versions must have these elements installed manually. The replication catalog may need to be installed for versions of Oracle earlier than 9i or if the database was manually created and all the catalog scripts were not run. The following query will help determine whether the catalog is installed.

```
SELECT COUNT(*)
FROM User_tables
WHERE Table_name LIKE 'REPCAT%';

COUNT(*)
--------
      43
```

Replication is already installed if there are table names that begin with *repcat$*.

If replication is not installed, it is easy and straightforward to install. The script to install the catalog is called *catrep.sql*, and it is located in the $ORACLE_HOME/rdbms/admin directory. It is highly recommended that invalid objects in the SYS and SYSTEM schemas be identified before and after installing the replication catalog. This script will generate a list of invalid objects.

```
SELECT
  owner,
  object_name,
  status
FROM
  dba_objects
WHERE
  owner IN ('SYS','SYSTEN')
AND
  status = 'INVALID';
```

Invalid packages can be recompiled with the *utlrp.sql* SQL script that is supplied with Oracle. This script is maintained in the $ORACLE_HOME/rdbms/admin directory on the database server. Packages can also be manually recompiled. Here is an example of calling the *utlrp.sql* script to recompile invalid database objects:

```
@?/rdbms/admin/utlrp.sql
```

Once all SYS and SYSTEM packages are valid, the replication objects can be installed. For version Oracle8i and earlier, use SVRMGRL and connect with INTERNAL. For version Oracle9i and later, use SQL*Plus to connect to SYS, using the "as sysdba" syntax as seen here:

```
C:>sqlplus "sys as sysdba"
```

Once connected, use the spool command to spool the output, otherwise the results will go flying by on the screen. To install replication, run *catrep.sql*. It is contained in the $ORACLE_HOME/rdbms/admin directory. Once that is done, turn off spooling, exit SQL*Plus, and then check the log file for any errors. Finally, verify that all SYS and SYSTEM packages are still marked valid.

 Invalid replication packages will make troubleshooting a replication problem much more complicated. You should fix the problem before you continue building the replication.

Oracle-Supplied Replication Packages

The following table lists the most commonly used replication packages, and the procedures and functions in those packages. Future chapters reference a number of these packages:

PACKAGE NAME	PURPOSE
dbms_defer	Provides an interface to allow procedure calls to be queued for later execution at remote nodes.
dbms_defer_query	Allows querying of deferred transaction queue data.
dbms_defer_sys	This is the administration interface into the deferred remote procedure call facility.
dbms_mview	This allows the analysis of the capabilities of existing, as well as proposed, materialized views. This procedure can also be used to refresh certain materialized views and to purge materialized view logs.
dbms_offline_og	This package contains the APIs required for offline instantiation of master groups.

PACKAGE NAME	PURPOSE
dbms_offline_snapshot	This package contains APIs required for offline instantiation of materialized views.
dbms_rectifier_diff	This package contains the APIs that can be used to determine if data inconsistencies exist between two replicated sites. It can then be used to resolve those inconsistencies.
dbms_refresh	Allows the creation and refreshing of groups of materialized views. This allows the group to be key-consistent to a specific point in time.
dbms_repcat	Allows the DBA to administer the replication environment.
dbms_repcat_admin	Allows the DBA to grant users the privileges required for advanced replication operations.
dbms_repcat_instantiate	Allows the DBA to instantiate deployment templates.
dbms_repcat_rgt	Allows the DBA to administer refresh group templates.
dbms_reputil	Provides a number of programs that allow management of the advanced replication environment.

Conclusion

The topics covered in this chapter include:

- Types of Replication.

- Setting up the Database for Replication.

- Database Links

- Replication Packages.

The topics in the remaining chapters progress from basic read-only replication through advanced multi-master replication. Monitoring replication environments and data contention will also be covered

At this point, the actual replication can be created. This first topic is basic replication, read-only materialized views.

Read-Only Materialized View Replication

Introduction to Read-only Views

This chapter will focus on read-only materialized view (Mview) replication, which is the least complex of the various replication methods. As the name implies, a read-only MView will not allow updates. As the Mviews refresh, the updates at the master site are propagated to the remote site.

For the purpose of terminology, the "local" site is the master site and the "remote" site of the destination for the replicated table.

On the remote site, the MViews allow access to the data but do not accept inserts, updates, or deletes. Use read-only materialized views when it is necessary to provide data that will support queries and reports at a separate location.

Here is a summary of the main topics in this chapter:

- Basic information on Mviews.

- Materialized View Logs.

- Updating data in Materialized Views

- Copying Mviews to other databases.

- Use of OEM to create Mviews.

- Refresh Groups for Materialized Views

- Creating Refresh Groups

- Refresh Groups with OEM

- Maintaining Read-Only Mviews

Materialized View Architecture

First, materialized views and the architecture surrounding them will be covered in more detail. The advantages that read-only materialized views offer will be considered, and a few administrative issues, such as altering and dropping materialized views will be examined.

Materialized Views

Oracle introduced the materialized view (Mview) in Oracle version 8 to replace snapshots. The materialized view is similar to a normal view, except it is a physical object that contains rows of data. When a normal view is created in the database, SQL is stored, rather than a physical table. However, with a materialized view, a physical object is created from data that no other object in the database contains.

An Mview can be used for two principle purposes. First, it can be used for replication, which is what will be reviewed here. An Mview can also be used as a means to denormalize database design, which is outside the scope of this book, but is nonetheless a very powerful feature. In both cases, Mviews can be used to improve the performance of Oracle databases.

Mviews are created via the *create materialized view* command, as seen in this example:

```
CREATE MATERIALIZED VIEW employees
AS
SELECT * FROM emp_user.employee@proddb;
```

Replicated Mviews come in the following forms:

- Primary key-based Mviews (the default)
- ROWID-based Mviews

These will now be explored in more detail.

Primary Key Based MViews

Primary-key Mviews are based on the primary key of the underlying table. Changes to a primary key Mview are propagated at the row-level. These changes are based on the primary key of the table, as opposed to the ROWID.

The following is an example of a SQL statement for creating a primary key materialized view:

```
CREATE MATERIALIZED VIEW employees AS
SELECT * FROM emp_user.employee@proddb;
```

Note that this particular Mview is not set up to refresh on any specific schedule; therefore it would need to be refreshed manually. A more complex implementation of an Mview will be covered later in this chapter.

ROWID-Based Mviews

Prior to Oracle8, all snapshots were based on ROWIDs, rather than primary keys. Snapshots are the precursor to Mviews. Newer versions of Oracle support ROWID materialized views for backwards-compatibility reasons. The ROWID Mview refreshes based on the ROWID of the master table. A ROWID Mview should only be used when the Mview is coming from an Oracle7 master table. ROWID-based Mviews are not recommended for Oracle8 and later databases.

The following is an example of a CREATE MATERIALIZED VIEW statement that creates a ROWID materialized view:

```
CREATE MATERIALIZED VIEW employees
REFRESH WITH ROWID AS
SELECT * FROM emp_user.employee@proddb;
```

Advantages of Read-Only MViews

Materialized views offer a number of advantages in a distributed computing environment, including:

- Reduction of network loads

- Improved performance on distributed systems

- Data subsetting

- No data conflicts

MViews reduce overall network traffic because queries that would have been distributed queries become local queries. This reduces network overhead. While there is some network overhead associated with the replication process, it is significantly less than with even a moderate volume of distributed queries.

Mviews offer enhanced performance on queries against distributed tables. Compared to queries using a database link, Mviews always offer faster response. Mviews also provide uninterrupted processing should the master site become unavailable. This is because the Mview is local in nature, and will be unaffected by the loss of the master site or the interconnecting infrastructure.

However, carefully consider the impact of data latency in the overall design, because loss of a component such as the network may mean that the data is in a divergent state, compared to the master site. This may or may not be a problem, depending on the particular requirements of the business.

Mviews also allow subsets of data to be provided at the remote site. Using the WHERE clause of the Mview, as well as selecting only specific columns, specific subsets of data can be made available at the remote site.

Finally, another benefit of read-only Mviews is the potential for data conflicts between the master and replicated sites is eliminated. This is not the case with updateable Mviews and advanced replication, which are covered in the next chapter.

Altering Mviews

The ALTER MATERIALIZED VIEW command can be used to modify an Mview. This command allows the DBA to change the refresh schedule or type of an Mview, or change the storage clause of an Mview. Here are some examples:

```
Alter materialized view enployee storage (next 100m);

ALTER MATERIALIZED VIEW employee
   REFRESH COMPLETE
   START WITH TRUNC(SYSDATE+1) + 9/24
   NEXT SYSDATE+7;
```

Dropping Mviews

Use the DROP MATERIALIZED VIEW command to drop an Mview that was previously created. Here is an example:

```
DROP MATERIALIZED VIEW employee;
```

Materialized View Logs

In most situations, the data in the Mview should be as current as possible. Also, many applications cannot tolerate data divergence, a difference between the data at the master site and the Mview site. Materialized View Logs (Mview Logs), created at the master site, allow Oracle to keep track of changes to the master table. Mview logs are created through the CREATE MATERIALIZED VIEW LOG command.

Mview Logs are used to apply row level changes to the remote Mview sites. Mview Logs can be created either on a table's primary key or on the table's ROWID. They can also be created on a combination of primary keys and ROWIDs.

The Mview log should be created on the primary key of the table whenever possible, as the use of the primary key involves fewer restrictions. In any case, materialized views used for replication must be rebuilt if the structure of the underlying table is changed.

Also, ROWID-based Mviews and Mview logs are impacted by reorganization and truncate operations on the source table. In the cases of reorganization and truncate operations, the Mviews built on that table will need to be completely refreshed.

Here is an example of the creation of an Mview Log based on the primary key (the default) of the master table:

```
Create materialized view log on employee tablespace users;
```

An example of the creation of an Mview log based on the tables ROWID:

```
Create materialized view log on employee
tablespace users
with ROWID;
```

And an example of the creation of an Mview log with both ROWID and primary key:

```
Create materialized view log on employee
tablespace users
with ROWID PRIMARY KEY;
```

The tablespace to create the Mview log should always be designated. If a tablespace is not specified, the Mview log's tablespace will default to the SYSTEM tablespace.

Some changes to the base table can invalidate materialized views, particularly if the log is created using ROWID. Like indexes, if the base table is rebuilt using the ALTER TABLE MOVE command, the relationship between row IDs and actual rows is changed, invalidating both indexes and materialized views based on that table. In this case, all of the table's indexes would have to be rebuilt, and a complete refresh on the materialized view would have to be executed. Similarly, if the master site database ever requires recovery, it is recommended that all replicated materialized views be completely refreshed.

Each replicated base table can have only one materialized view log. If the base table is replicated to multiple remote locations, all of the remote materialized views will refresh from the same Mview log, in addition to any local materialized views using the base table.

Updates, inserts, and deletes on the base tables cause changes in the row information to be placed in the materialized view logs. As each remote materialized view refreshes, it will pull the information from the logs it needs to update itself. Once all remote sites have refreshed, the old data is removed from the materialized view log.

Once an Mview log is created, there will be some additional tables created in the schema that owns the Mview log. These tables are the materialized view logs.

```
select table_name from dba_tables
where table_name like 'MLOG%' or
table_name like 'RUPD%';

SQL> select table_name from dba_tables
  2  where table_name like 'MLOG%' or
  3  table_name like 'RUPD%';

TABLE_NAME
------------------------------
RUPD$_EMPLOYEE
MLOG$_EMPLOYEE
```

The *mlogs$_<table_name>* is the materialized view log created with the CREATE MATERIALIZED VIEW LOG command. Note that materialized view log tables using primary keys also have *rupd$_* tables, as is the case in this example. The *rupd$_* table supports updateable materialized views, which are only possible on log tables with primary keys.

The materialized view logs are just like any other table and can be queried.

```
SQL> desc mlog$_bonus;
 Name                                    Null?    Type
 --------------------------------------- -------- -------------
 M_ROW$$                                          VARCHAR2(255)
 SNAPTIME$$                                       DATE
 DMLTYPE$$                                        VARCHAR2(1)
 OLD_NEW$$                                        VARCHAR2(1)
 CHANGE_VECTOR$$                                  RAW(255)
```

Execute a *select count(*)* to determine whether there are changes waiting to propagate.

```
SQL> select count(*) from mlog$_bonus;

  COUNT(*)
----------
         0

1 row selected.
```

In this case, there are no rows waiting to propagate.

Updating Mview Data

Mviews for replication are updated based either on a specific replication schedule or on demand. A refresh interval is defined when the materialized view is created on the remote site. Oracle automatically creates a job to execute the refresh at the defined interval. To create an Mview with a scheduled refresh, use the REFRESH FAST syntax, as demonstrated in the next example:

```
CREATE MATERIALIZED VIEW employees
REFRESH FAST NEXT sysdate + 1 AS
SELECT * FROM emp_user.employee@proddb;
```

This will cause an Mview called "employees" to be created. The Mview will be fast-refreshed every day at roughly the same time.

There are two other refresh methods that can be selected when creating an Mview. The following table provides details about all three:

REFRESH METHOD	DESCRIPTION	NOTES
Fast	Causes replication based on row level changes.	Requires an Mview log be created at the master site.
Complete	Causes the entire Mview to be refreshed, rather than just specific row changes.	The Mview will be truncated and then repopulated. This implies that it will become unavailable for a period of time.
Force	Causes a fast refresh to occur if that is possible. If a fast refresh is not possible, then a complete refresh will be performed.	This option avoids replication failures if the source table should not be fast refreshable.

When an Mview is scheduled for replication, a related job is created in the Oracle job scheduler. Issuing the following query will show this job.

```
Select job, what, failures from dba_jobs where what like
'%dbms_refresh%';
```

Ensure that the job scheduler is properly configured. Specifically, ensure that the parameter *job_queue_process* is set to a value greater than 0. Setting the *job_queue_process* will enable one or more different job scheduler threads. These threads can and do run in parallel - set them carefully or there will be so much parallel activity that the database is brought to its knees.

If the refresh fails for any reason, including problems with the database link or the master database site, the job will log a failure in the *dba_jobs* column FAILURE and reattempt the refresh after a period of time. Normally, a job will attempt to re-execute one minute after the first failure, then two minutes after the second failure, four minutes after the third failure, and so on until it reaches either 16 failures or the time reaches the refresh interval.

If the refresh interval is every two minutes, the job will reattempt to execute one minute after the first failure and will reattempt to execute every two minutes after that until it reaches 16 failures. When a job reaches 16 failures, it marks itself as broken (as seen in the BROKEN column of *dba_jobs*) and makes no further attempt to execute. Once a job successfully executes, it resets its number of failures to zero.

If a job becomes broken, the problem must be fixed, and then the *dbms_job.broken* procedure is used to reset the job to active status. To tell if a replication job is operating, look at the *dba_jobs_running* view. This view provides a list of all currently executing jobs.

The *dbms_refresh.refresh* procedure can be used to manually refresh an Mview. Here is an example of refreshing the example employee's Mview:

```
dbms_refresh.refresh('"SYS"."EMPLOYEES"');
```

Replicating Schemas with Materialized Views

Many shops replicate entire schemas to a remote site. In this case, a simple script will assist in the creation of the materialized view logs. The script below will generate the commands to create the materialized view logs for schema replication.

🖫 cr_mview_logs.sql

```
--
--      Copyright © 2003 by Rampant TechPress Inc.
--
--      Free for non-commercial use.
--      For commercial licensing, e-mail info@rampant.cc
--
-- ***********************************************
set pages 0 line 130, feedback off
-- Using Primary Keys
spool mview_logs_pk.sql
select
   'create materialized view log on '|| table_name ||
   'tablespace users using primary key;'
from
  user_tables
where
  table_name in (
    select
      table_name
    from
      user_constraints
    where
      constraint_type = 'P')
;
spool off

-- using rowids
spool mview_logs_rowid.sql
select
```

```
from
  user_tables
where
  table_name not in (
    select
      table_name
    from
      user_constraints
    where
      constraint_type = 'P')
;
spool off
```

Review the two scripts (*mview_logs_rowid.sql* and *mview_logs_pk.sql*) and remove any table that is not being dynamically replicated. The scripts generated will look like the following, when executed in the SCOTT schema.

```
mview_logs_pk.sql
create materialized view log on DEPT tablespace users with primary
key;
create materialized view log on EMP tablespace users with primary
key;

mview_logs_rowid.sql
create materialized view log on BONUS tablespace users with rowid;
create materialized view log on SALGRADE tablespace users with
rowid;
```

Remove any table not being replicated and run the scripts to create the materialized view logs.

A similar script can be used to create the Mviews on the remote site.

```
select
  'create materialized view '|| table_name ||
  'using primary key refresh force next sysdate +1 as   \
   select * from '|| table_name ||'@navdb.world;'
from
  user_tables
where
  table_name in (
    select
      table_name
    from
      user_constraints
    where
      constraint_type = 'P')
;
```

Spool the results to a file so they can be edited to remove tables that do not require replication, and then run the script on the remote site. Do the same with tables that have no primary key and must use ROWIDs.

Creating Materialized Views using OEM and DBConsole

There's a saying among ancient DBAs, "Real men don't use GUIs." It can be modified slightly to say "Smart men use GUIs if it makes the task easier." For the purposes of replication, GUIs are helpful as long as everything works. However, when problems arise, the GUIs hide the details and often prevent identification of the problem. That being said, Oracle Enterprise Manager could be an easy way to check the status of the replication. If something needs to be fixed, do it in SQLPLUS.

At one time Oracle Support did not recommend creating replication with OEM because it would continue to run after encountering an error, and then report that everything completed successful, when in fast it had failed. As of 9iR2, Oracle Support actually recommends the use of OEM because there is less likelihood of making mistakes and OEM better handles errors during the creation process.

For those hard-core DBAs who insist on using GUIs, here is an example of creating a replicated materialized view using Oracle Enterprise Manager (OEM). The example uses the OEM version that comes with Oracle9iR2. OEM for Oracle9i is similar, but the version in Oracle8i is not very useful. Regardless of the database version, use the OEM that comes with Oracle9iR2.

To start OEM on Windows, go to the START menu and find the Oracle Enterprise Manager Console. On UNIX/LINUX, open a terminal window as the oracle user (or a user with the oracle ENV set up) and enter "*oemapp console*". If the database is not listed in OEM, click on the database icon and select Add Databases To Tree. The database can be added manually or through the server *tnsnames.ora* file.

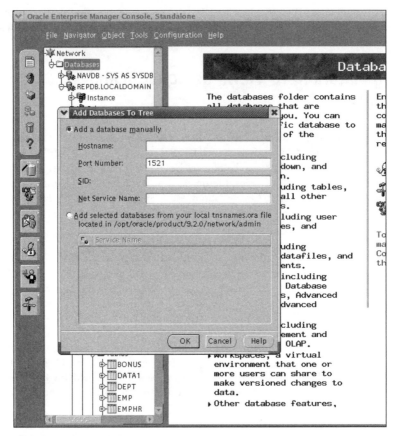

Figure 3.1: *Adding a Database to OEM*

Log on to the remote database as the SYSTEM user; the user SCOTT does not have enough privileges to use with OEM. Select schema, then SCOTT. If user SCOTT does not contain any objects, he will not be listed under schemas. In that case, use the SYSTEM schema. Right click and hold on SCOTT (or SYSTEM) and select create. A window will open listing all the creation options.

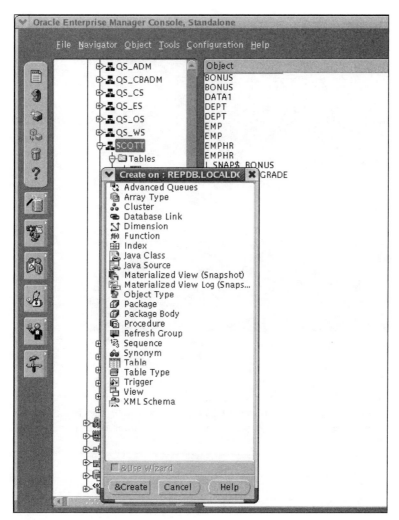

Figure 3.2: *Creating Objects in OEM*

Select Materialized View and press the Create button at the bottom. The Create Materialized View window will open. If the session began in SYSTEM, ensure that the schema is changed to SCOTT. Provide the Mview name (in this case EMP) and ensure the correct tablespace is selected. Clear the query rewrite checkbox and enter the materialized view query in the text box provided: "*select * from scott.emp@navdb.world*".

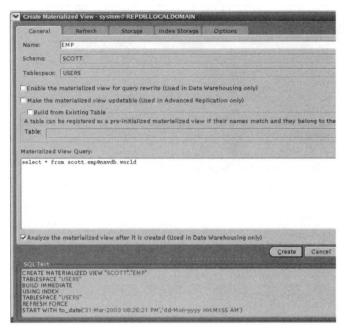

Figure 3.3: *Create Materialized View in OEM*

Now select the REFRESH tab. Check the Populate Immediately box. Select the refresh method that defaults to FORCED. Drop down to the Refresh Interval. Select "automatically," the sysdate is shown and then the interval. Select 3 minutes in the text box.

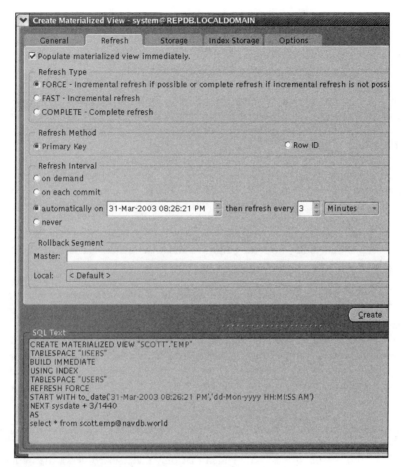

Figure 3.4: *Setting the Refresh Interval in OEM*

At the bottom of the window, select "Show SQL" to see the actual command OEM will execute when Apply is pressed. Press the Apply button and answer OK when OEM warns that query rewrite is off and that Populate may take time. If all goes well, a window will indicate that the materialized view was created.

Refresh Groups for Materialized Views

The tables are available for use once the database replication is completed. The next step is to insure the integrity of the data between materialized views. An example will illustrate how things can go awry without refresh groups.

Suppose the home office (master site) updates everyone's salary. The remote site operates with a refresh interval of 3 minutes. Every 3 minutes the replicated tables are updated. At the remote site, a clerk is generating salary checks. To create a check, the clerk joins the employee table with the salary table.

The clerk may find an employee that has no entry in the salary table. This cannot happen at the master site because of the presence of a foreign key. However, at the remote site, the employee table has just finished a refresh but the salary table will not refresh for 2 more minutes.

If a foreign key were placed between the employee and salary tables at the remote site, the salary table would always have to refresh before the employee table to avoid violation of the foreign key. The answer to this dilemma is to create a refresh group.

A refresh group refreshes all materialized views in the group together. By creating a refresh group and including both the employee and salary materialized views, the data integrity between the materialized views is maintained.

Refresh groups are created and maintained using the *dbms_refresh* package. There are a few practical limitations on refresh groups. The number of materialized views that can be in one refresh group is limited by the time required to execute the refresh. If a refresh group is created with 100 replicated materialized views, the time it takes to refresh the 100 views will probably be prohibitive. None of the tables in the refresh group will be available during the long refresh. Especially with replicated materialized views, consideration must be given to the amount of time it takes to refresh across the network.

Another concern is the amount of redo/undo information generated during a refresh. A refresh group will generate more redo/undo than individual materialized views. For this reason, it is recommended that only materialized views that require referential integrity be placed into groups. Allowing the remainder of the materialized views to refresh on their own will reduce blocking waits caused by the refresh.

Creating Refresh Groups

Refresh groups are created using *dbms_refresh.make*. To create a refresh group called REP_GROUP1 for the replicated materialized views EMP AND DEPT, use the following commands.

```
BEGIN
   DBMS_REFRESH.MAKE(
      name => '"SCOTT"."REP_GROUP1"',
      list => '',
      next_date => SYSDATE,
      interval => '/*3:Mins*/ sysdate + 3/(60*24)',
```

```
            implicit_destroy => TRUE,
            lax => FALSE,
            job => 0,
            rollback_seg => NULL,
            push_deferred_rpc => FALSE,
            refresh_after_errors => TRUE,
            purge_option => NULL,
            parallelism => NULL,
            heap_size => NULL);
END;
/
```

The command above creates an empty refresh group in the SCOTT schema called
REP_GROUP1. Materialized views could be added using the MAKE command by
listing them in the *list* parameter, such as:

```
list=>'emp,dept'
```

The interval is set to 3 mins. The *implicit_destroy* clause determines whether the
refresh group is deleted when the last object is removed. In this case, when objects
are added and later deleted, REP_GROUP1 will be removed when the last object is
removed.

The *lax* clause is used when adding materialized views to the refresh group. A
materialized view can only be in one refresh group. If the command had contained
the materialized view SCOTT.EMP in the list clause, and SCOTT.EMP was already
in another refresh group, the *lax* clause would have to be set to TRUE. The
materialized view SCOTT.EMP would be moved from the current refresh group to
REP_GROUP1. If the *lax* clause were FALSE then SCOTT.EMP would remain in
its current refresh group.

To add materialized views to RE_GROUP1, use the *dbms_refresh.add* procedure.

```
BEGIN
   DBMS_REFRESH.ADD(
      name => '"SCOTT"."REP_GROUP1"',
      list => '"SCOTT"."DEPT"',
      lax => TRUE);
END;
/
BEGIN
   DBMS_REFRESH.ADD(
      name => '"SCOTT"."REP_GROUP1"',
      list => '"SCOTT"."EMP"',
      lax => TRUE);
END;
/
```

Both materialized views EMP and DEPT are added to REP_GROUP1. Because the
lax clause is TRUE, if either view belonged to another refresh group, they would be
added to REP_GROUP1 and deleted from the other group. Notice that the views

---

are in the list clause. The same results could be obtained using the following command:

```
BEGIN
   DBMS_REFRESH.ADD(
     name => '"SCOTT"."REP_GROUP1"',
     list => '"SCOTT"."EMP","SCOTT"."DEPT"',
     lax => TRUE);
END;
/
```

To remove SCOTT.DEPT from REP_GROUP1, use the *dbms_refresh.subtract* procedure.

```
BEGIN
   DBMS_REFRESH.SUBTRACT(
     name => '"SCOTT"."REP_GROUP1"',
     list => 'SCOTT"."DEPT"',
     lax => FALSE);
END;
/
```

If a materialized view is removed from a refresh group without being placed in another group, it will be placed in its own refresh group.

The *dbms_refresh* package handles the jobs that execute the refresh groups. When a materialized view is added to a refresh group, the job that was used to refresh the view is removed and the new refresh group's job will execute the refresh.

 Warning - When a materialized view is placed in a refresh group, it will be refreshed at the interval set in the group, not in the materialized view. For example, if a materialized view is created with a refresh interval of 3 mins and is then placed in a refresh group with an internal of 5 mins, the materialized view will refresh every 5 mins.

However, the interval setting in the materialized view will still be 3 mins. Once the materialized view is removed from the refresh group it will again refresh at 3 mins. This causes confusion, especially when using OEM, because the materialized view indicates it is refreshing every 3 mins when in fact it is not.

The CHANGE procedure in the *dbms_refresh* package should also be mentioned. The most common change is the refresh interval.

```
BEGIN
   DBMS_REFRESH.CHANGE(
      name => '"SCOTT"."REP_GROUP1"',
      next_date => SYSDATE,
      interval => '/*5:Mins*/ sysdate + 5/(60*24)');
END;
/
```

Here, the next execution date is set to SYSDATE (in other words, NOW) and the interval is set to 5 mins. To change the interval without changing the data, use NULL instead of SYSDATE. NULL will cause the current setting to be maintained. Since these parameters really just set the conditions for a job, they can be set to any function acceptable to *dbms_job*.

Refresh Groups with Oracle Enterprise Manager

OEM excels at creating and maintaining refresh groups. To find refresh groups, open OEM and sign on to the database. Expand the following sections: Distribution →Materialized View Replication → Materialized View Site → Refresh Groups. There is a refresh group for each materialized view.

To create a refresh group and add the EMP and DEPT materialized views, simply right-click and hold the Refresh Group tab or the SCOTT schema. Select Create, then select Refresh Group, and press Create.

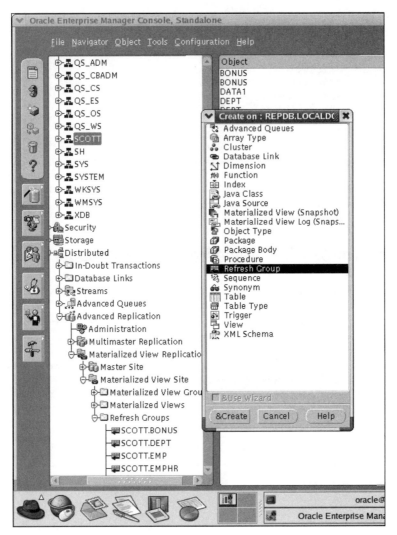

Figure 3.5: *Creating a Refresh Group with OEM*

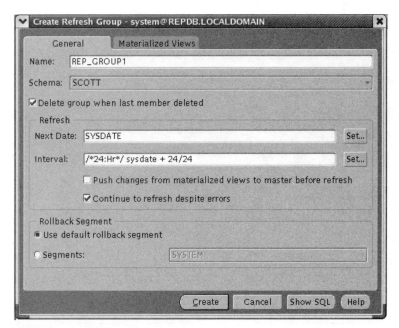

Figure 3.6: *Creating a Refresh Group*

Name the refresh group "Refresh Group1" and select SCOTT as the Schema. Mark the checkbox to delete the group when the last member is deleted. Also, mark the checkbox to continue to refresh despite errors.

Next, press the Set button to set the refresh interval.

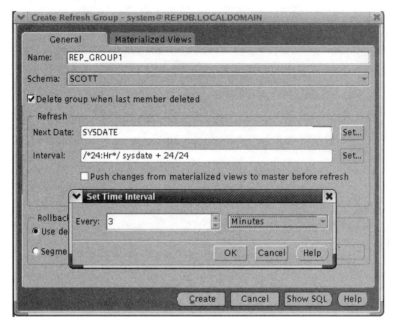

Figure 3.7: *Setting the Refresh Interval*

Select the interval level in the combo box on the right, and then enter a number in the text field. Select Create and the interval is set on the main window.

Now, select the Materialized Views Tab. An empty window opens to add the materialized views. Select ADD and Add Materialized View(s) in the refresh group window. Select the SCOTT schema to see the list of materialized views belonging to SCOTT. Select EMP and DEPT and select Add to move them to the bottom window. Select OK, and the materialized views appear in the materialized views windows. Press Create and wait for the success dialog box.

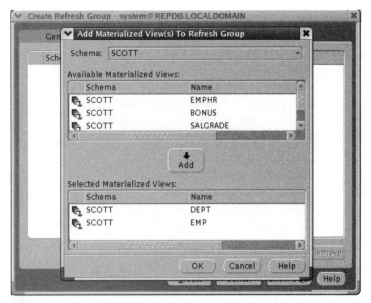

Figure 3.8: *Adding Materialized Views to the Refresh Group*

It is also simple to add or remove materialized views from the refresh groups. Select Refresh Groups under the Distribution Section. Right-click and hold on the Refresh Group to modify and select View/Edit Details. This is the same window used to create the refresh group. Select the Materialized View Tab to get a list of the views currently in the group. To remove a view, select it and press remove. The view disappears from the window and the APPLY button appears. Press Apply to remove the view. To add a view, press the Add button and follow the procedure covered above.

Maintaining Read-only Materialized Views

Maintaining replicated materialized views primarily involves keeping the jobs running. If the network goes down or the base site is not available, the jobs that support replication will eventually break. To restart the replication, just restart the job. To find broken jobs, select from *dba_jobs* or *user_jobs*.

```
Select
  job,
  schema_user,
  what
from
  user_jobs
where
  broken = 'Y';
```

There are two methods to fix broken jobs. Either use the *dbms_job.run* procedure to execute the job immediately and reset the broken flag, or use the *dbms_job.broken* procedure to reset the flag and let the job run at the next interval.

```
execute DBMS_JOB.RUN(23);

execute DBMS.JOB.BROKEN(23,FALSE, SYSDATE + 5/(24*60));
```

This can be embedded into a script to automate the processes.

```
unbroken.sql

spool run_unbroken.sql
select
    'exec dbms_job.broken('||job||',FALSE,sysdate + 1/288);'
from
    user_jobs
where
    broken != 'N';
spool off
@run_unbroken.sql
```

The script must be run in the schema that contains the refresh groups, since jobs can only be modified by the schema that creates them. Even SYS can't run a job created by another schema. A script can be created to run *unbroken.sql* periodically to repair broken jobs.

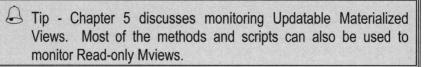

Tip - Chapter 5 discusses monitoring Updatable Materialized Views. Most of the methods and scripts can also be used to monitor Read-only Mviews.

Oracle Enterprise Manager is pretty good at giving an overview of replicated objects, even read-only materialized views. Under the Distributed option, open Advanced Replication and select Administration. OEM checks the status of the replication and produces a chart depicting the type of replication on the database. Arrows depict the direction of dataflow between the systems. Notice the arrow points from the remote site to the base site. This depiction becomes more useful as the replication becomes more complicated. For now, select the JOBS tab to see all jobs on the system. This includes all jobs in the database.

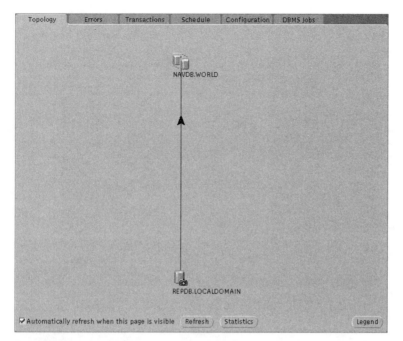

Figure 3.9: *Advanced Replication Administration with OEM*

The list of jobs shows that Job 2 is currently broken. The DBA must be logged in as SCOTT to fix Job 2.

Figure 3.10: *Jobs Status in OEM*

Highlight Job 2 and press the Edit button at the bottom of the window.

The Edit Job window opens with the current job parameters. Select Normal from the Status combo box and press the OK button. Next Date and Interval can also be changed. Once back at the Jobs Status window, press the Apply button to execute the changes.

Figure 3.11: *The Edit Job Window*

Conclusion

That's all there is to read-only materialized view replication. The basic information was covered in this chapter, materialized view logs were examined, and updating and copying Mviews to other databases was reviewed. Another topic covered was how the Oracle Enterprise Manager can aid in creating Mviews, and how Refresh Groups are used with materialized views.

The next chapter will introduce updateable materialized views, used for two-way replication between a remote site and a single master site.

Updatable Materialized Views

Updatable Materialized Views (UMV) are a type of multi-master replication available in Oracle 8.1 and later. In this chapter, UMVs will be introduced and then a description of how to set up systems to use UMVs will be provided. The chapter concludes with a look at how OEM fits into the UMV picture.

Introducing Updatable Materialized Views

Chapter 3 covered how an ordinary one-way Materialized View (Mview) allows for replication of data from a master site to one or more remote sites. Mviews allow replication of data from one table, multiple tables, or the pre-aggregation of information from many base tables into a summarized materialization of the base tables. As shown in Figure 4.1, one-way MV technology allows a Materialized View to be refreshed in several ways.

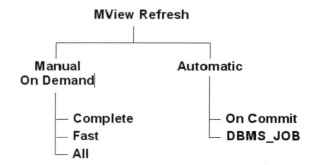

Figure 4.1: *Updating a One-Way Materialized View*

Updatable Materialized Views are different because they allow the replicated Materialized View to be updated. Figure 4.2 displays how Oracle accomplishes this by having the replicated Mview "push" changes back to the master table and then "pull" changes from the master table materialized view log.

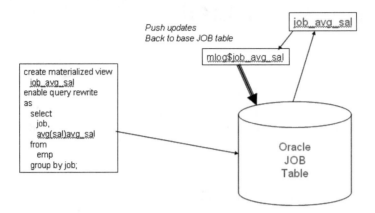

Figure 4.2: *Updating an Updatable Materialized View*

A UMV is far more sophisticated than an ordinary MV and quite a bit more powerful. The features of UMV technology include:

- Support for numerous sites - One master table can support as many UMVs as the hardware and bandwidth will allow.

- Easy conflict resolution - Since there is only one master table in the UMV replication architecture, all conflict resolution is consolidated into one Oracle system.

- Low resource usage - UMVs require fewer resources than master-to-master multi-master replication and still allow the master site to replicate with other master sites.

UMVs are used when the replicated databases only replicate with one master database. (Figure 4.3) This is a great approach for non-distributed systems but fails if there are multiple master sites.

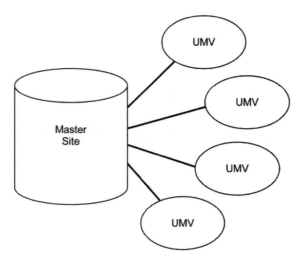

Figure 4.3: *Single Master Updatable Materialized View*

For systems that contain multiple master databases (such as global distributed Oracle systems), updatable materialized view replication can be integrated into a replication scheme that includes multiple master databases (Figure 4.4).

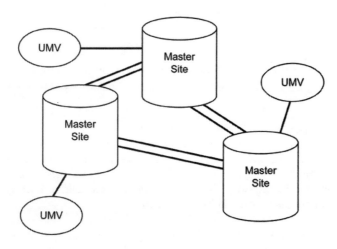

Figure 4.4: *Multiple Master Updatable Materialized Views*

In the multiple master schemes, each UMV site replicates with only one master site, while the master sites use multi-master replication to pass changes between each other.

The next section takes a closer look at the steps needed to implement UMV technology.

Setting-up Updatable Materialized View Replication

Chapter 2 introduced how UMVs are a form of advanced replication. The replication packages must be installed on both databases, unless version 9i or later is being used, in which case the packages are installed automatically.

For the purposes of this book three standard users will be used to facilitate replication, as well as the schema owner PUBS on both the master and remote sites. The users can be named anything, however, these names are usually standardized: REPADMIN and REPPROXY. In older databases, these names may be SNAPADMIN and SNAPPROXY.

Creating Users on the Master Site

On the master site, the user REPADMIN is the replication administrator. Replication is created through this user and all maintenance must be performed using the REPADMIN user. The user REPPROXY assists propagation and security on the master site by acting as a proxy for access to the master tables.

On the UMV Site, the user REPADMIN is the replication administrator. All replication and replication maintenance must be performed through the REPADMIN user.

The REPADMIN user on the UMV database will do the actual communication with the master database thru the REPPROXY user ID. Replication is set up this way for security reasons so that users will not have access to the actual master tables. This was explained in more detail in Chapter 2, *Installing Oracle Advanced Replication*. It is important not to change the passwords for these users once replication is set up as replication will stop until the database links are updated.

Multi-master replication in Oracle 8.1.5 and above uses the master-view methodology. First, a master site, is defined containing at least one replication group. This database will be called *navdb* for purposes of this example. Objects are added to the replication group and replication support is generated and started. At this point, the master site maintains information on all the objects in the replication group to support replication.

Users on the Remote Site

On the remote site, where the UMVs will be created within a database called MYDB, a materialized view group is defined with a link to one and only one replication group. Materialized views are generated in the materialized view group and are marked as updatable. These materialized views operate as normal materialized views in relation to the base table, except they are not read-only. Inserts, updates, and deletes are propagated back to the master site base table. Changes to the UMVs, such as Inserts, Updates, and Deletes, can be propagated back to the master site asynchronously or synchronously.

Asynchronous propagation is preferred because it significantly speeds up the commits, however, a method must be created to resolve the problem of collisions on primary keys caused by simultaneous changes.

Asynchronous propagation queues changes and sends them to the master site periodically (every 1 min for example), just as one-way replication refreshes. The change to the UMV might violate the primary key of the base table when Oracle tries to apply the change to the base table. This situation is known as a *collision*. Rules will need to be defined to deal with collisions when configuring UMVs.

The master replication group on the master database can support many UMV sites, however, each materialized view group on the UMV database can only replicate from one master replication group.

Advanced replication can be a complex beast. Thus, the setup for advanced replication operations can be fairly complex. It is important that each step be accomplished in sequence and the success of that step verified.

In the following examples, the replicated tables have primary keys, and it is strongly suggest that only tables that have primary keys are replicated. There is a method to replicate a table without a primary key – it consists of instructing Oracle to use a column or columns as the key. This method actually defines a primary key within the replication to use in collision detection and can have unexpected impacts on data added to the table. Therefore, it is recommended to always define a primary key on tables to be replicated.

Extra step for Oracle 8i and lower

With Oracle version 8i and lower, the script *catrep.sql* you will need to be run before using any advanced replication functionality. This script is located in the *$ORACLE_HOME/rdbms/admin* directory and should be run through SVRMGR1 connected as internal.

Step 1: Insure initSID.ora parameters are correct

This insures that there are enough resources to support multi-master replication. Recommended parameters should be set on both the master and UMV sites unless noted.

PARAMETER NAME	DEFAULT VALUE	RECOMMENDED VALUE
compatible	Depends on the version of Oracle that is being used.	Set *compatible* to the version of Oracle that is being used in order to use all replication features of that version of the database
distributed_ transactions	.25 * the parameter setting for transactions	Add 5 + 2 per master to the existing value. Note this is obsolete in Oracle9i and later.
global_names	FALSE	It is required to set *global_names* to TRUE in each database that will be involved in advanced replication.
job_queue_ processes	0	This parameter must be set to a value of at least one. Higher values will allow more parallel replication of objects.
open_links	4	*open_links* defines the number of concurrent database links that are required to a given database. This parameter needs to be configured for an initial setting of 4 + 2 additional links for each master site.
parallel_ automatic_ tuning	FALSE	Oracle9i offers this parameter to help establish the correct level of parallelism. Set to TRUE to allow Oracle to determine the best configuration for parallel operations.
parallel_max_ servers	Derived based on the parameters: *cpu_count, parallel_ automatic_ tuning, parallel_ adaptive_ multi_user*	This is only important for parallel propagation, which is recommended. This parameter's value should be configured high enough to allow sufficient parallel servers to be started. Generally, the default is sufficient.
parallel_min_ servers	0	Set this value to the number of parallel streams that are expected.
processes	Derived from the value of the parameter *parallel_max_ servers*	Only set on the UMV site. Should be set high enough to allow all Oracle related processes to operate. Add to an existing database one process for each UMV that will be replicated. Note that master sites do not need additional processed added.

PARAMETER NAME	DEFAULT VALUE	RECOMMENDED VALUE
replication_ dependency_ tracking	TRUE	Should be set to the default value.
shared_pool_ size	OS Dependent	Generally will need to be increased for replication environments. Generally adding 20m for basic replication and 40m for advanced replication is sufficient.

Table 4.1: *Recommended Parameter values*

The above *initSID.ora* parameters are required for the replication and should be added or modified in the remote UMV databases as required.

All replicated databases, master sites, and UMVs must have unique global names. To determine a database's global name use:

```
select * from global_name;
```

Global names are established when the database is created and can be changed via the ALTER DATABASE command using the RENAME *global_name* clause, as seen in this example:

```
Alter database rename global_name to mydb.world.outdomain.com;
```

Step 2: Verify (or Install) the Replication Packages

Multi-master replication requires that the *catrep.sql* package be installed at both the master site and the UMV site. Oracle 8i does not install replication support by default, but Oracle 9i and later automatically installs the replication packages. Replication support must be installed on both the master site and the UMV site. Part of installing replication support is insuring that all packages are successfully compiled.

```
select
  owner, object_name
from all_objects
where status = 'INVALID';
```

This code lists all packages that require recompiling. All SYS and SYSTEM packages must be compiled before starting replication. If a SYS or SYSTEM package is marked invalid, log into SYS and recompile all invalid package bodies that can be recompiled with the Oracle supplied script *utlrp.sql*, which can be found in the *$ORACLE_HOME/rdbms/admin* directory.

Once replication support is installed and all SYS/SYSTEM packages are compiled, replication support can be set up.

Step 3: Setup the Master Site Users

The master site requires two users. The first user is called REPADMIN. REPADMIN handles all replication administration. The second user is called REPPROXY. REPPROXY is the user that interacts with the remote UMV sites. For this demonstration, part of the PUBS schema will be replicated. PUBS is a teaching schema that supports book publication.

On the UMV site, the one required user is called REPADMIN. This user is the replication administrator. All replication and replication maintenance must be performed using the REPADMIN user.

In this example, the task is to replicate a set of tables supporting book sales, which include the *book* table (primary key BOOK_KEY), the *store* table (primary key STORE_KEY), and the *sales* table (no primary key). These tables need to be replicated to the *mydb* database. This example will use updatable materialized views.

Because replication is built into the Oracle kernel, parameters have to be loaded so that it will function. The following scripts look non-intuitive, however, most of them simply load the parameters to be used by the replication code.

First, set up the master site.

All Scripts are available in the CODE Depot

Step 3.1: Create the REPADMIN User

cr_repadmin.sql creates the user REPADMIN and establishes the necessary direct grants. The grants must be direct and not via a ROLE. It also loads the REPADMIN user into *repcat_admin* to administer replication on any schema.

Note: Depending on how the database was created, there may already be a REPADMIN schema. If that is the case, there is no need to run the CREATE USER command, but the remaining commands should be run.

🖫 create_repadmin.sql

```
--
--   Copyright © 2003 by Rampant TechPress Inc.
--
--   Free for non-commercial use.
--   For commercial licensing, e-mail info@rampant.cc
--
-- *************************************************
```

```
    identified by repadmin;
alter user repadmin default tablespace users;
alter user repadmin TEMPORARY tablespace temp;
grant connect, resource to repadmin;
grant comment any table to repadmin;
grant lock any table to repadmin;
```

Step 3.2: Create the REPPROXY User

The script below creates the user REPPROXY and establishes the necessary direct grants. The grants must be direct and not via a ROLE. Lastly, it registers REPPROXY as a "proxy_repadmin" which is a proxy for REPADMIN on UMV sites to allow REPADMIN to create materialized views and as a "receiver" to receive changes propagated from the UMV sites. From Chapter 2, REPPROXY is using the trusted model.

🖫 create_snap_proxy.sql

```
--
--     Copyright © 2003 by Rampant TechPress Inc.
--
--     Free for non-commercial use.
--     For commercial licensing, e-mail info@rampant.cc
--
-- ************************************************

create user repproxy
  identified by repproxy;
alter user repproxy default tablespace users;
alter user repproxy temporary tablespace temp;
grant create session to repproxy;
grant select any table to repproxy;
--
--
BEGIN
  dbms_repcat_admin.register_user_repgroup(
    username =>        'repproxy',
    privilege_type => 'proxy_repadmin',
    list_of_gnames => NULL);
END;
/
BEGIN
  dbms_repcat_admin.register_user_repgroup(
    username =>        'repproxy',
    privilege_type => 'receiver',
    list_of_gnames => NULL);
END;
```

The next step is to create the replication users on the UMV site.

Step 4: Setup the UMV Site Users

As the UMV site requires, two users will be created. First, the REPADMIN user will be created to administer replication and perform all maintenance at the site. A schema called PUBS will also be set up where the actual UMVs will be created. This schema should be named exactly the same as the master site schema. The replication schemas must have the same name but can and should have different passwords for security reasons.

Step 4.1: Create REPADMIN User

The script below creates the user REPADMIN and establishes the necessary direct grants. The grants must be direct and not via a ROLE. Because REPADMIN will administer all replication activities on the UMV site, the next step is to register REPADMIN with *repcat_admin* to administer any schema. REPADMIN is also registered as a propagator. Lastly, some direct grants are established on the PUBS schema.

🖫 create_snap_admin.sql

```
--    Copyright © 2003 by Rampant TechPress Inc.
--
--    Free for non-commercial use.
--    For commercial licensing, e-mail info@rampant.cc
-- ************************************************

connect system/????@mydb
create user repadmin
  profile default
  identified by repadmin
  default tablespace users
  temporary tablespace temp
  account unlock;

grant alter any materialized view to repadmin;
grant create any materialized view to repadmin;
grant connect to repadmin;
grant comment any table to repadmin;
grant lock any table to repadmin;

execute dbms_repcat_admin.grant_admin_any_schema('repadmin');
execute dbms_defer_sys.register_propagator('repadmin');

create user pubs
```

```
   default tablespace users
   temporary tablespace temp
   account unlock;

grant connect, resource to pubs;
grant create table to pubs;
```

Step 5: Create Database Links

Database links are required only from the UMV site to the master site. All replicated
databases must have unique global names. Since REPPROXY is the entry point into
the master database, the private links will connect to REPPROXY. *mydb* will need
two private links, one for REPADMIN and the other for PUBS.

The first step is to create a public link using the master site's global name, *navdb.world*,
to the entry in the *tnsnames.ora* file (Net 8 alias), which is *navdb*. Next, a private link is
created from REPADMIN to REPPROXY to allow replication requests to be
passed, and finally, from PUBS to REPPROXY to build the UMVs.

`cr_dblinks.sql create the links.`

Step 5.1: *Create the public link with the UMV Database*

```
connect SYSTEM/passwd@mydb.world

create public database link navdb.world
  using 'NAVDB';
```

Step 5.2: *Create a private user link*

Create the private link from REPADMIN to REPPROXY using the public link
mydb.world.

```
connect repadmin/repadmin@mydb

create database link navdb.world
  connect to repproxy identified by repproxy;
```

Next, check the link.

```
select * from dual@navdb.world;
```

The result will produce the letter X in the D column if the link worked:

```
D
X
```

Step 5.3: Create a private database link

Lastly, create a private database link from PUBS to REPPROXY.

```
connect pubs/pubs@mydb

create database link navdb.world
  connect to repproxy identified by repproxy;
```

Next, check the link.

```
select * from dual@navdb.world;
```

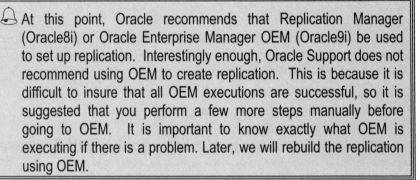

At this point, Oracle recommends that Replication Manager (Oracle8i) or Oracle Enterprise Manager OEM (Oracle9i) be used to set up replication. Interestingly enough, Oracle Support does not recommend using OEM to create replication. This is because it is difficult to insure that all OEM executions are successful, so it is suggested that you perform a few more steps manually before going to OEM. It is important to know exactly what OEM is executing if there is a problem. Later, we will rebuild the replication using OEM.

Step 6: Create the Materialized View Log

A materialized view log must be created on each of the UMV replicated tables. Here is an example of the use of the CREATE MATERIALIZED VIEW LOG command to create an Mview log:

```
create materialized view log on pubs.store
tablespace users
with primary key
including new values;
```

Before creating the Mview log, define a primary key for the *sales* table. If one has not been defined, the following error message will be generated:

```
create materialized view log on pubs.store
*
ERROR at line 1:
ORA-12014: table 'STORE' does not contain a primary key constraint
```

Step 7: Create the Master Replication Group

Each UMV must be part of a master replication group and must have an identifiable primary key. Trying to create a UMV without a primary key being defined will fail.

If the UMV does not have a defined primary key, a materialized view will be created instead of a UMV. This is a special kind of materialized view, as it can be updated. The data changes made to the materialized view will be lost with every refresh of new data from the master, effectively resulting in a one-way system of replication.

The primary key may be defined from a single column or multiple columns. If there is no set of columns that defines a primary key, then it is common practice to establish a pseudo (or surrogate) primary key for that table (such as a sequence number). The *sales* table happens to have a column that can be defined as a primary key, the ORDER_NUMBER column.

Cr_master_rep_gp.sql creates the master replication group REP_GP1 and adds the *store* table. It then generates replication support for the STORE table object. Finally, it starts replication support for the REP_GP1. This is run on the master site.

The script can be accessed from the online code depot.

> 🖫 **cr_master_rep_gp.sql**

Step 7.1: Create the master replication group REP_GP1

Use the *dbms_repcat* stored procedure called *create_master_repgroup* to create the master replication group. This group must be configured before UMV replication will be possible.

```
connect repadmin/repadmin@navdb

begin
  dbms_repcat.create_master_repgroup(
    gname => '"REP_GP1"',
    qualifier => '',
    group_comment => '');
end;
/
```

Step 7.2: Add the STORE table from the PUBS schema to the master replication group

Now, use the *dbms_repcat* procedure called *create_master_repobject* to add the *store* table to the master replication group that was just created.

```
begin
  dbms_repcat.create_master_repobject(
    gname =>  '"REP_GP1"',
    type =>   'TABLE',
    oname =>  '"STORE"',
    sname =>  '"PUBS"');
end;
/
```

Step 7.3: Generate replication support for the STORE table object

Once the table is added to the master replication group, replication support needs to be generated for it. The *generate_replication_support* procedure within the *dbms_repcat* package provides the facilities to do that. This command loads the object into the internal tables and creates the functions and procedures needed for replication support.

```
begin
  dbms_repcat.generate_replication_support(
    sname =>  '"PUBS"',
    oname =>  '"STORE"',
    type =>   'TABLE',
    min_communication => TRUE);
end;
/
```

At this point, check the view DBA_REPCATLOG for errors.

```
Select count(*) from dba_repcatlog;
```

This view should be empty.

If *dba_repcatlog* is empty, start replication activity on the master site. If *dba_repcatlog* is not empty, then wait and recheck. When the database has created the replication support for the table, the *dba_repcatlog* view should be empty.

Step 7.4: Add the remaining two tables to the replication group

If everything has gone according to plan, the *store* table is now being replicated. Now, repeat this process for the *book* and *sales* tables as well:

```
connect repadmin/repadmin@navdb
begin
  dbms_repcat.create_master_repobject(
    gname => '"REP_GP1"',
    type =>  'TABLE',
    oname => '"BOOK"',
    sname => '"PUBS"',
    copy_rows => TRUE);
end;
/
begin
  dbms_repcat.generate_replication_support(
    sname => '"PUBS"',
    oname => '"BOOK"',
    type =>  'TABLE',
    min_communication => TRUE);
end;
/

BEGIN
   DBMS_REPCAT.CREATE_MASTER_REPOBJECT(
     gname => '"REP_GP1"',
     type => 'TABLE',
     oname => '"SALES"',
     sname => '"PUBS"');
END;
/

begin
  dbms_repcat.generate_replication_support(
    sname => '"PUBS"',
    oname => '"SALES"',
    type =>  'TABLE',
    min_communication => TRUE);
end;
/
```

Step 7.5: Notify the master (NAVDB) database to track activity on the REP_GP1 objects by resuming replication activity

Replication is set up, so it's time to see it in action. From the master database, use the *resume_master_activity* procedure within *dbms_repcat* to start the replication process:

```
begin
  dbms_repcat.resume_master_activity(
    gname => '"REP_GP1"');
end;
/
```

The master site (NAVDB) is now waiting for the UMV site to begin replication. As changes are made to the UMV or to the master table, they will be propagated as required.

The view *dba_repgroup* can be used to check the status of the replication groups that are created. After creating the replication groups and generating the replication support for various tables within that group, query the *dba_repgroup* table to insure that REP_GP1 status field is set to "Normal" as seen in this example:

```
SQL> select sname, master, status from dba_repgroup;

SNAME                           M STATUS
------------------------------- - ---------
REP_GP1                         Y NORMAL
```

With the master site now tracking changes to the PUBS base tables, the updatable materialized views can be created on the *mydb* (remote) database.

Step 8: Create the Updatable Materialized View at the Remote Database

IMPORTANT: Log onto the UMV site as REPADMIN, not as PUBS.

Step 8.1: Create a Refresh Group

First, a refresh group needs to be created on the remote database so that all three UMVs will refresh together. Notice that *push_deferred* and *refresh_after_errors* are set to TRUE. Setting *push_deferred_rpc* tells the refresh group that updates will be pushed back to the master table. Setting *refresh_after_errors* to true will allow the UMVs to continue to refresh, even if there are errors in the DEFERROR queue.

```
BEGIN
  DBMS_REFRESH.MAKE(
    name => '"REPADMIN"."GROUPA"',
    list => '',
    next_date => SYSDATE,
    interval => '/*1:Mins*/ sysdate +
      1/(60*24)',
    implicit_destroy => FALSE,
    lax => FALSE,
    job => 0,
```

```
        rollback_seg => NULL,
        push_deferred_rpc => TRUE,
        refresh_after_errors => TRUE,
        purge_option => NULL,
        parallelism => NULL,
        heap_size => NULL);
END;
/
```

Step 8.2: Create the Materialized View Group

Now, create the materialized view group in the MYDB database. In order for UMVs to push changes back to the master tables, the UMVs must belong to a materialized view group.

```
BEGIN
    DBMS_REPCAT.CREATE_MVIEW_REPGROUP(
        gname => '"REP_GP1"',
        master => 'NAVDB.WORLD',
        propagation_mode => 'ASYNCHRONOUS');
END;
/
```

This creates a replication group called REP_GP1 on the UMV database that uses the *mydb.world* database link. It will propagate data asynchronously.

Step 8.3: Create the BOOK Updatable Materialized View

The next step is to create the actual materialized view on the remote site. Here, the BOOK materialized view is created:

```
CREATE MATERIALIZED VIEW "PUBS"."BOOK"
REFRESH FAST FOR UPDATE
AS SELECT * FROM "PUBS"."BOOK"@MYDB.WORLD c
```

In this CREATE MATERIALIZED VIEW statement, the table names need to be fully qualified since a UMV is being created in the PUBS schema as the REPADMIN user. The option also exists to create and use private or public synonyms, instead of fully qualifying.

Restrictions could also have been placed on the columns in the UMV by specifying which columns to include, or restricting the rows with a WHERE clause. Here is an example of that type of materialized view:

```
CREATE MATERIALIZED VIEW "PUBS"."BOOK"
REFRESH FAST FOR UPDATE
AS SELECT isbm_number, name, publisher
FROM "PUBS"."BOOK"@MYDB.WORLD c
```

Step 8.4: Add the Book UMV To the Refresh Group

Since the desired result is to have the UMVs to replicate together, the BOOK updatable materialized view is added to the refresh group GROUPA.

```
BEGIN
    DBMS_REFRESH.ADD(
      name => '"REPADMIN"."GROUPA"',
      list => '"PUBS"."BOOK"',
      lax => TRUE);
END;
/
```

Step 8.5: Update The UMV Replication Group

Now, the BOOK updatable materialized view is added to the materialized view replication group REP_GP1 that was created earlier. This creates the replication support needed for two-way replication with the master site. The BOOK updatable materialized view is now replicating with the *book* base table on the master database.

```
BEGIN
    DBMS_REPCAT.CREATE_MVIEW_REPOBJECT(
        gname => '"REP_GP1"',
        sname => '"PUBS"',
        oname => '"BOOK"',
        type => 'SNAPSHOT',
        min_communication => TRUE);
END;
/
```

Step 8.6: Add Other UMVs

Now follow steps 8.3 through 8.5 to add the other two updatable materialized views (Sales and Store).

```
CREATE MATERIALIZED VIEW "PUBS"."SALES"
REFRESH FAST FOR UPDATE
AS SELECT * FROM
"PUBS"."SALES"@NAVDB.WORLD;

CREATE MATERIALIZED VIEW "PUBS"."STORE"
REFRESH FAST FOR UPDATE
AS SELECT * FROM
"PUBS"."STORE"@NAVDB.WORLD;

BEGIN
    DBMS_REFRESH.ADD(
      name => '"REPADMIN"."GROUPA"',
      list => '"PUBS"."SALES"',
      lax => TRUE);
```

```
END;
/

BEGIN
   DBMS_REFRESH.ADD(
      name => '"REPADMIN"."GROUPA"',
      list => '"PUBS"."STORE"',
      lax => TRUE);
END;
/

BEGIN
   DBMS_REPCAT.CREATE_MVIEW_REPOBJECT(
      gname => '"REP_GP1"',
      sname => '"PUBS"',
      oname => '"SALES"',
      type => 'SNAPSHOT',
      min_communication => TRUE);
END;
/

BEGIN
   DBMS_REPCAT.CREATE_MVIEW_REPOBJECT(
      gname => '"REP_GP1"',
      sname => '"PUBS"',
      oname => '"STORE"',
      type => 'SNAPSHOT',
      min_communication => TRUE);
END;
/
```

At this point, all three updatable materialized views are replicating with the base tables on the master site. The updates on the master table will be replicated to the UMV, and updates to the UMV will be replicated back to the master table.

 Bug Alert! There is a bug in Oracle9i that fails to update the dba_mview with the correct status. The compiled_state will show 'INVALID' and the refresh fields will be incorrect. A check of the updatable materialized view will show that it is in fact valid and is refreshing IAW the refresh interval of the assigned refresh group.

The last two areas to cover are monitoring UMV replication and establishing methods to resolve primary key collisions. These subjects will be covered in Chapters 5 and 7.

This chapter so far has covered how to manually create the updatable materialized views, now it's time to bring in Oracle Enterprise Manager to simplify these operations.

Creating Replication Using OEM

Once UMV replication is running, it is easy to update and monitor it using Oracle's Enterprise Manager. OEM is a powerful tool that gets better with each release. However, one problem with using OEM in building replication is that it performs a number of steps at once, without fully insuring that each step completes successfully.

This can sometimes result in a report of a successful execution while, in fact, some part did not complete successfully. In practice, the object will not replicate successfully and it will be difficult to determine the cause. For this reason, use the method above to manually create replication on at least one table, and then use OEM to add additional objects to the replication.

The following sections build UMV replication using OEM and continue the previously described Steps beginning at Step 5 using OEM.

It is still necessary to load the replication schemas into *dbms_repcat_admin*, so these tasks will be executed using the scripts already provided. The process will pick up with OEM at step 5, creating the database links. Since OEM does multiple steps, these steps will not be exactly identical to the previous group of steps.

The master site is still called NAVDB and the UMV site is still MYDB. Both are Oracle9iR2 databases, so the replication catalog is already installed.

Step 5 - Create the Database Links

After logging onto MYDB as the SYSTEM user, create a public database link by selecting the "Distributed" tab, right clicking on the "Database Link" folder, and selecting Create. The master database SID is NAVDB, which is also the Net Service Name in the *tnsnames.ora* file (Figure 4.5).

Figure 4.5: *Creating a public database link*

Be sure to select the public checkbox. Selecting the "SHOW SQL" button will cause OEM to display the SQL that will be used to execute the command. Select OK to execute the command and create the database link. OEM displays a dialog box to confirm that the link was created (Figure 4.6).

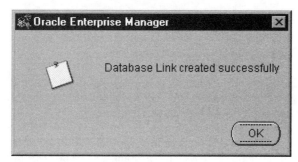

Figure 4.6: *Database Link Creation Dialog Box*

Next, log on as REPADMIN to create the private database link. To log onto OEM as REPADMIN, REPADMIN will need to be granted the system privilege

"SELECT ANY DICTIONARY." Navigate back to the Database Link folder, right-click, and select Create. Create the private database link from REPADMIN to REPPROXY (Figure 4.7) using the same link name as the private link created above.

Figure 4.7: *Create a Private Database Link*

Again, OEM displays a dialog box confirming the creation of the link. Next, test the link by expanding the Database Link folder, selecting the database link under the REPADMIN user. Select the "Test" button and OEM will verify that the link is active.

Step 6 - Create the Master Replication Group

Now, log onto the Master database (*navdb*) as REPADMIN. Again, it is necessary to grant "SELECT ANY DICTIONARY" to REPADMIN in order to log on with OEM. Expand the Distributed tab and the Advanced Replication tab.

This is the area of OEM that will be used to perform most of the replication maintenance. Expanding the Multi-master Replication folder will display the Master Groups folder. Now, right-click on the folder and select "Create".

In the Name field enter the name of this replication group, REP_GP1. Select the Objects tab and select ADD. Here, the *book* table is going to be added from the PUBS schema. Use the schema dropdown menu to select the PUBS schema. Check the "Tables" check box and a list of tables is provided. Select the *book* table and press the "ADD" button. The *book* table is now listed in the "Selected Objects" text area (Figure 4.8).

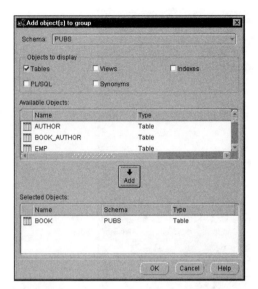

Figure 4.8: *Selecting Replication Objects in OEM*

Select OK to return to the Objects tab, which now displays the *book* table. Selecting the "Show SQL" button shows the series of commands that this step will execute. This one step will generate the master replication group, add the *book* table to the group, generate the replication support, and finally resume replication activity (Figure 4.9).

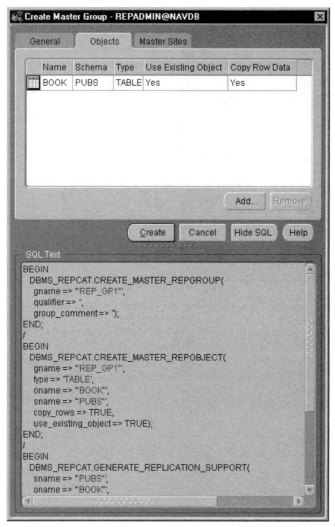

Figure 4.9: *OEM Create Master Group*

Selecting "Create" will cause OEM to execute the commands and create the master replication group. Once created, the master group folder and the REP_GP1 tab can be expanded to see the PUBS.BOOK table. Selecting the REP_GP1 tab will display the status page.

This demonstrates how Oracle has used the graphic capabilities of OEM to combine multiple steps for simultaneous execution. The commands out of the "Show SQL" text field can be highlighted and copied to save as a file, which can be very helpful when problems arise.

The next steps deviate from the steps introduced in the first part of this chapter and add the *sales* and *store* tables in the PUBS schema to the master group. Before adding additional tables to the replication group, replication activity needs to be stopped.

From the REP_GP1 status page (Figure 4.10), select the "Submit Stop Request" button in the Replication Activity section. Notice that the status changed from Running (Normal), to Stopped (Quiesced). Select the Objects tab and then select the Add button at the bottom.

If OEM requests that an "alternate key column" be set on the *sales* table, then the primary key hasn't been set. Selecting a column or columns will define a key for use in replication that cannot be used to create a UMV.

Select the Apply button to add the new tables. Next, highlight the new tables and press the "Generate Replication Support" button.

Return to the General page and restart replication activity. The status should return to Running (Normal) (Figure 4.10).

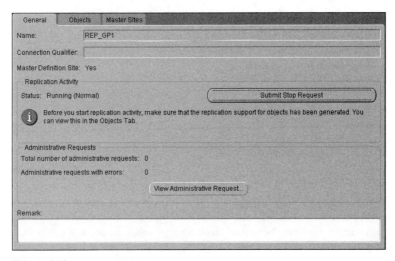

Figure 4.10: *Restarting Replication Support*

Now, all the tables to be replicated in the PUBS schema are generating replication support and the Updatable Materialized Views can be created in the *mydb* database.

Step 7 - Create the Updatable Materialized Views

Now that master replication is running normally, it is time to create the updateable materialized views.

Log onto the UMV site as REPADMIN. In this example, that is the *mydb* database. Again, expand the Distributed tab, the Advanced Replication tab, and in this case, the Materialized View Replication tab (Figure 4.11).

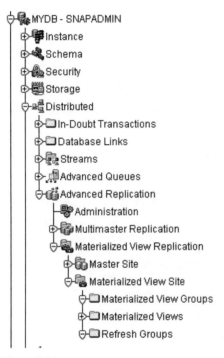

Figure 4.11: *OEM Materialized View Replication*

As with creating UMVs manually, the first step using OEM is to create a materialized view group. Right-click on the Materialized View Groups folder and select "Create using Wizard."

The first thing the wizard asks for is the database link. Select the "All" checkbox to see the available database links. Select the one that was created at the start of this section, in this case *navdb.world* (Figure 4.12).

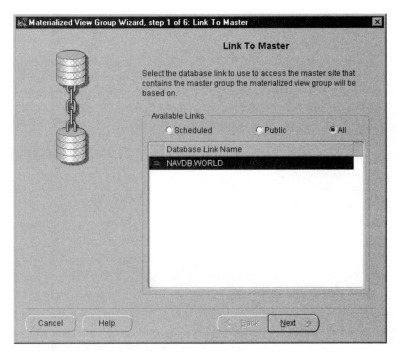

Link To Master

Select the database link to use to access the master site that contains the master group the materialized view group will be based on.

Available Links

○ Scheduled   ○ Public   ◉ All

Database Link Name
NAVDB.WORLD

Cancel   Help   Back   Next

Figure 4.12: *Mview Group Wizard Link to Master*

Selecting the "Next" button will display the Master Groups page. Notice that the master replication group that was created on the master database, *navdb*, is listed. The wizard polled the *dba_repcat* data dictionary view across the link to locate the available master replication groups.

If an error is generated the text area does not display the name of the master group, then the "SELECT ANY DICTIONARY" system grant may need to granted to REPPROXY on the master database. Stop the wizard and restart it to display the list of master groups (Figure 4.13).

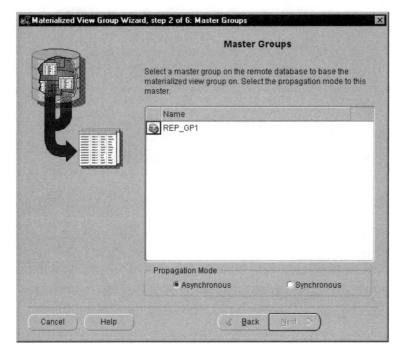

Figure 4.13: *Mview Group Wizard Master Groups*

Now, leave the Asynchronous radio button set and select the master group, which is REP_GP1 in this example. When "Next" is selected, the wizard will use the database link to get a list of replication objects contained in the selected group. In this case, it is the three tables that are replicated from the PUBS schema (Figure 4.14).

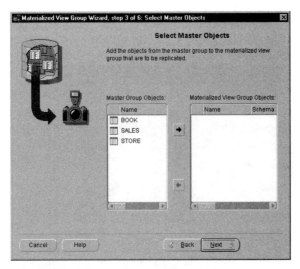

Figure 4.14: *Mview Wizard Select Master Objects*

Since all three tables are being replicated to the *mydb* database, use the right-arrow to move the three tables to the Materialized View Group Objects side.

There is no requirement that the UMV site replicate all the objects in the master group. It is not uncommon for some sites to replicate a subset of the objects. As with all parts of replication, more is not better, if it's not needed, don't replicate it.

As each table is moved, the wizard gathers more information across the database link. Selecting Next will display the Materialized View Defaults page.

Now a Refresh Group needs to be created. In the *mydb* database, there are currently no refresh groups defined, so the drop down box is grayed out. If the database contains refresh groups, then they will be displayed in the drop down box. It is recommended that a new refresh group be created rather than mixing the UMVs with other materialized views.

It is also recommended that the UMVs be separated from any one-way Mviews on the database. Although over one hundred Mviews can be placed in a refresh group, remember that one process refreshes all members of the group and holds locks on tables during the refresh process.

Experience shows that a number of smaller refresh groups works best because the task is spread across more job processes. The only requirement that must be considered when grouping objects in refresh groups is that they may depend on each other and they must refresh together to ensure data integrity.

Selecting the Create button will bring up the Create Refresh Group page (Figure 4.15).

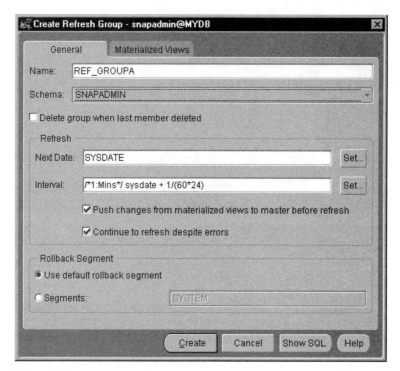

Figure 4.15: *Create Refresh Group*

The refresh group is named REF_GROUPA. Make sure that the REPADMIN schema is selected from the Schema combo-box. If the refresh group should be deleted when the last object is removed, select the checkbox.

Change the refresh interval by pressing the Set button. Here, the refresh interval is set to 1 min. Because this refresh group will support UMVs, select the "Push changes..." and "Continue to refresh..." checkboxes. Select the "Show SQL" button to see the actual SQL used to create the refresh group.

If the Materialized View tab is selected at the top of the window, a list of all available materialized views will be visible. However, the views in the master replication group will not be shown because they do not yet exist in the *mydb* database. So, without adding Mviews, select Create. OEM will display a dialog box showing that the refresh group was created and the display will return to the Materialized View Defaults page (Figure 4.16).

Figure 4.16: *Materialized View Defaults*

Select the first three check boxes. To explicitly define a storage clause, check the fourth check box and then the Edit button to define the storage parameters.

Selecting Next advances to Step 5 of the wizard and allows the customization of any of the UMVs before creation. As each name is selected, the checkboxes on the right will change to show the current setting.

If the Fast Refresh check box cannot be set, it is because the materialized view log on that table has not been created. The wizard will need to be cancelled, the objects dropped in *mydb*, and the table will need to be removed from the Master Group in *navdb*. Then, create the materialized view log and add the table back to the master group. Restart the wizard on *mydb* (Figure 4.17).

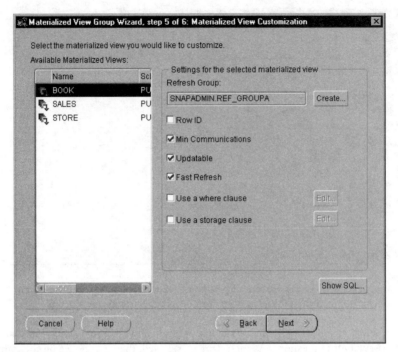

Figure 4.17: *Materialized View Customization*

This page of the wizard also allows the incorporation of a WHERE clause in the updatable materialized view to restrict the rows included in the view.

Selecting Next takes advances to the last step. Check the box in the center of the window to record a script of what OEM is about to execute. The script is important because if the creation fails, it can be used to locate problems.

Selecting Finish will produce a list of the objects that will be created (Figure 4.18).

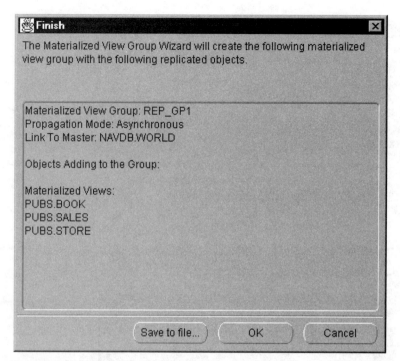

Figure 4.18: *Rollup of Objects Being Created*

When OK is selected, OEM will create all the objects. After finishing, the script can be saved to a file. Again, this is important when tracking down any problems, so it it is strongly suggested that the script be saved(Figure 4.19).

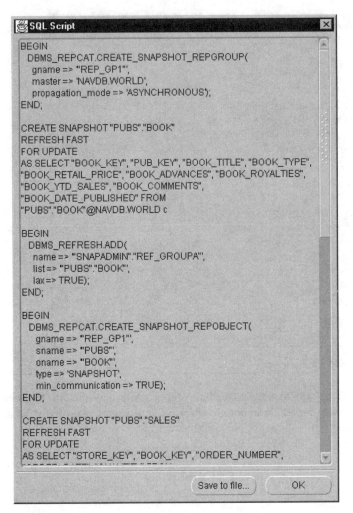

```
SQL Script                                            ☒

BEGIN
  DBMS_REPCAT.CREATE_SNAPSHOT_REPGROUP(
    gname => "REP_GP1",
    master => 'NAVDB.WORLD',
    propagation_mode => 'ASYNCHRONOUS');
END;

CREATE SNAPSHOT "PUBS"."BOOK"
REFRESH FAST
FOR UPDATE
AS SELECT "BOOK_KEY", "PUB_KEY", "BOOK_TITLE", "BOOK_TYPE",
"BOOK_RETAIL_PRICE", "BOOK_ADVANCES", "BOOK_ROYALTIES",
"BOOK_YTD_SALES", "BOOK_COMMENTS",
"BOOK_DATE_PUBLISHED" FROM
"PUBS"."BOOK"@NAVDB.WORLD c

BEGIN
  DBMS_REFRESH.ADD(
    name => "SNAPADMIN"."REF_GROUPA",
    list => "PUBS"."BOOK",
    lax => TRUE);
END;

BEGIN
  DBMS_REPCAT.CREATE_SNAPSHOT_REPOBJECT(
    gname => "REP_GP1",
    sname => "PUBS",
    oname => "BOOK",
    type => 'SNAPSHOT',
    min_communication => TRUE);
END;

CREATE SNAPSHOT "PUBS"."SALES"
REFRESH FAST
FOR UPDATE
AS SELECT "STORE_KEY", "BOOK_KEY", "ORDER_NUMBER",

              [ Save to file... ]    [    OK    ]
```

Figure 4.19: *Saving the Wizard Produced Script*

Replication is now functioning. To test, simply add or change data in the UMV, and after the refresh interval, verify that the data was replicated to the master table.

OEM provides an Advanced Replication Administration section. Under Advanced Replication, select the Administration tab. This will display a topography page that provides a graphic depiction of the replication and also shows errors, if present, in red in the DEFERROR queue.

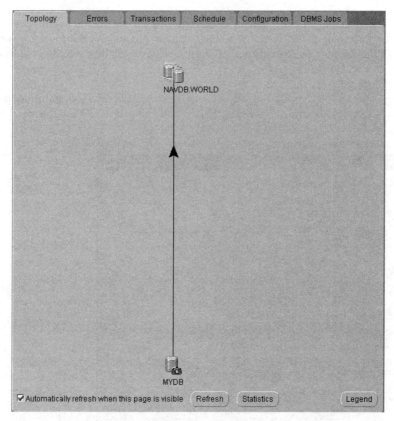

Figure 4.20: *Advanced Replication Administration Page*

This shows that the Mviews are on *mydb* and that they are replicating with *navdb*. In UMV, replication errors will normally be generated at the master site and will be shown in red.

The DBMS Jobs tab is displayed in the upper right. This is the only place OEM displays jobs and the only place they can be changed. Since UMV replication requires jobs to function, this section can be used to verify and maintain the replication jobs (Figure 4.21).

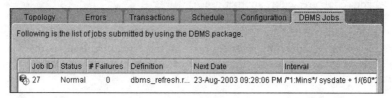

Figure 4.21: *OEM dbms_jobs Page*

To verify that the job is still functioning, confirm that the Next Date has not passed. The jobs background processes sometimes stall or get stuck behind a lock, and current time will pass the Next Date. Monitoring UMVs will be covered in the next chapter.

To change the refresh interval or other job properties, select the job and press the Edit button at the bottom of the page. This will bring up the Edit Job window (Figure 4.22).

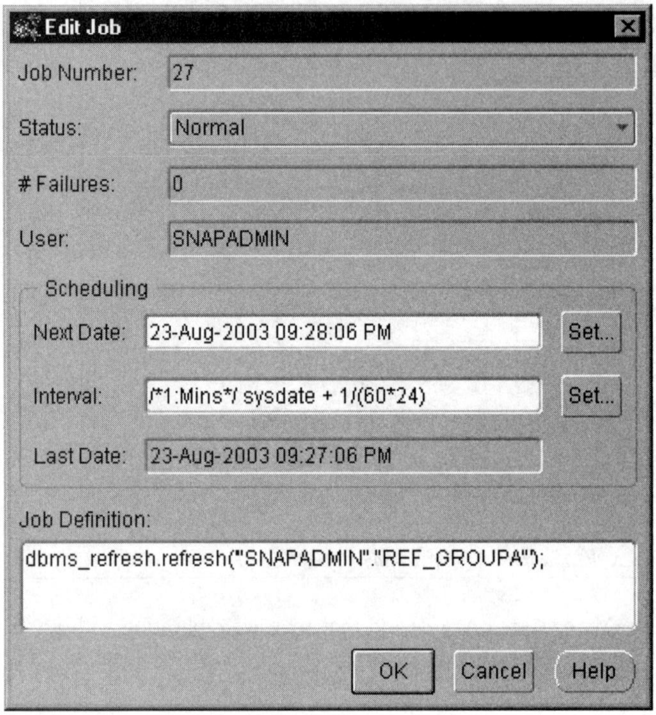

Figure 4.22: *The Edit Job Window*

Make any necessary changes and select OK. If OEM will not allow modification of a job, it is because the user needs to be logged on as the job's creator. Even SYS cannot change a job created by another user.

Now the updatable materialized view replication is running, it needs to be kept running. Since background job processes perform this type of replication, there are a number of problems that can stop the replication. Monitoring UMVs will be covered in Chapter 5.

Conclusion

This chapter has introduced the concept of Updatable Materialized Views (UMV) and described the steps to create a UMV using scripts and Oracle Enterprise Manager (OEM). The main points of this chapter include:

- A UMV offers significant advantages over a one-way materialized view because it allows interactive two-way updating.

- Features include:

  - Lower resource consumption

  - Easy conflict resolution

  - Number of UMVs limited only by hardware and bandwidth

- Discussion of the steps involved in creating UMVs using scripts.

Chapter 5, *Monitoring Materialized Views*, will cover creating a system that will check the status of the replication and, if possible, automatically fixing it.

Replication
Monitoring

Monitoring is a hallmark operation for any mission-critical enterprise database. Since replication is an important part of the overall enterprise data distribution schema, replication operations must be monitored carefully for any problems that may occur.

The first stop in this chapter will be the job scheduler. Both one-way replication and updatable materialized views rely on the database job scheduler to execute jobs that refresh the materialized views. Next, methods are introduced to monitor the replication job processes to ensure that replication continues to function, or if problems are encountered, to generate an alert to notify the administrator that intervention is required.

The Oracle Job Scheduler

It is important to understand the job scheduler and how it works because Oracle uses the job scheduler to refresh the data within the Oracle Mviews. From the DBA's perspective, it's important to ensure that replication jobs are not broken, which implies that they are failing. A broken job will halt the updates of the Mviews causing the data in the Mview to become stale. The next section looks at the job scheduler in a bit more detail.

A Refresher on the Oracle Job Scheduler

The Oracle job scheduler is an internal database process that allows jobs to be scheduled within Oracle. Oracle provides the *dbms_job* package and Oracle views to manage the job scheduler.

Within the job scheduler, a job can execute any procedure or function that is accessible. Each job is executed using an Oracle background process. The number of available concurrent background processes is defined by the database initialization parameter *job_queue_processes*.

```
JOB_QUEUE_PROCESSES = 5
```

When the database is started, the number of job queue processes defined by *job_queue_processes* will start.

In Oracle9i, a job queue coordinator process (CJQO) is spawned at database startup as well. On a regular basis, the CJQO checks for jobs that are ready to run within the job scheduler. By default, this check occurs every 5 seconds.

One of the benefits of the job scheduler architecture is that it allows for the execution of parallel Oracle jobs, which can be a very powerful feature if used correctly. However, caution must be taken not to enable too many job queue processes as this can burden the system. It is recommended that no more than one job queue process be enabled per CPU.

A background process executes a job as the user that defined the job. In other words, the process assumes the privileges of the user that created the job. The process will not have any privileges that the job creator does not possess.

If the job executes successfully, it will be rescheduled according to the interval that was established when the job was created. For example, the interval may be defined as sysdate + 1, which would indicate that the next job execution should be scheduled to occur the next day.

If the job scheduler fails to execute a job, the failure is recorded. Failures continue to increment until 16 failures are reached. At that point, Oracle will break the job and suspend future executions. The DBA will then have to intervene to "unbreak" the job.

Note: For a complete treatment of Oracle job scheduling, see Dr. Hall's (Oracle ACE of the Year, 2006) book "*Oracle Job Scheduling*".

Using dbms_job

The *dbms_job* package can be used to administer jobs within the users' own schema. The *dbms_job* package permits the user to:

- "Break" or "Unbreak" a job using the *dbms_job.broken* procedure.

- Change the interval between jobs with the *dbms_job.interval* procedure.

- Change the next execution date for a job with the *dbms_job.next_date* procedure.

- Remove an existing job using the *dbms_job.remove* procedure.

- Run an existing job using the *dbms_job.run* procedure.

- Add a job using the *dbms_job.submit* procedure.

- Query the job scheduler for the description of the job with the *dbms_job.what* procedure.

Note that when using *dbms_job*, only the user that created the job has the ability to change or delete the job. However, privileged accounts such as SYS can use the *dbms_ijob* package to administer any job in the system. Most of the procedures in *dbms_job* are in *dbms_ijob*, though some parameters may differ. An example of a procedure that is not in *dbms_ijob* is the CHANGE procedure.

 Commit! In some versions of Oracle (it also appears to be version specific) a commit may need to be executed after an execution of the dbms_job command. If calls to dbms_job do not appear to be working, try issuing a commit afterwards.

Creating a Replication Job

In both one-way and updatable materialized view replication, the required jobs are automatically created. However, creating a job is relatively easy. The code below will create a job that executes a STATSPACK snapshot every 5 min.

```
DECLARE jobno number;
BEGIN
  DBMS_JOB.SUBMIT(job => jobno,
                what => 'statspack.snap',
                next_date => SYSDATE,
                interval => '/*5:Mins*/ sysdate + 5/(60*24)'); END;
/
```

Note that *dbms_job.submit* returns the job number, so a variable will need to be defined to catch it. The same thing can be accomplished in Oracle Enterprise Manager. Navigate to the Distributed, Advanced Replication, Administration tab and select the DBMS Jobs tab at the top to display any jobs already defined. Select the NEW button at the bottom to define a new job.

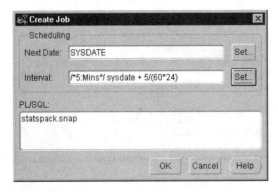

Figure 5.1: *The Create Job Screen*

Define the Next Date, Interval, and a PL/SQL procedure, function, or text to execute and select OK.

Deleting a Job

To delete a job, the job number should be known and the user who created the job will need to be logged in and execute the following script.

```
BEGIN
  DBMS_JOB.REMOVE(job => 1);
END;
/
```

This will remove a job with a job identifier of 1. The job identifier can be extracted from the *dba_jobs* view, which will be covered later in this chapter. If an error is generated that the job is not in the job queue, then the job's creator is not logged in to perform this process or the job does not exist.

Changing a Job

To change a table that is refreshing every 5 minutes to refresh every 15 minutes, adjust the interval in the supporting job.

```
BEGIN
  DBMS_JOB.CHANGE(job => 1,
    next_date => SYSDATE,
    interval => '/*15:Mins*/ sysdate +
              15/(60*24)',
    what => NULL);
END;
/
```

By changing the *next_date* to SYSDATE, the job will execute immediately, and then every 15 minutes after that. Setting the WHAT field to null in the above example will cause the field to retain its current value.

Stopping a Job

Stopping a job is also easy. Each job has a field called BROKEN. If this field is true, the job is broken and will not execute until it is unbroken.

```
BEGIN
  DBMS_JOB.BROKEN(job => 1, broken => TRUE); END;
/
```

Job 1 is now broken and will not execute. To restart Job 1, BROKEN must be reset to false and the Next Date must be reset. When a job is broken, the Next Date is set to 01 Jan 4000.

```
BEGIN
  DBMS_JOB.CHANGE(job => 1,
                 next_date => SYSDATE,
     interval =>'trunc(SYSDATE+1/24,'HH')',
                 what => NULL);
END;
/
BEGIN
  DBMS_JOB.BROKEN(job => 1,
                 broken => FALSE);
END;
/
```

The first step uses *dbms_job.change* to reset the *next_date* and *interval* parameters. *next_date* will be the next time the job will actually run. *interval* will determine when the job will be scheduled for its next execution after *next_date* arrives and the job executes. The second step uses *dbms_job.broken* to set the broken flag of the job to FALSE, thus allowing it to be scheduled once again.

Monitoring Replication Jobs

Monitoring jobs is a relatively simple process. The Oracle database maintains a data dictionary view called *dba_jobs* that contains the status of all jobs executing in the database. Here is a description of the *dba_jobs* view:

```
SQL> desc dba_jobs
 Name            Null?    Type
 --------------- -------- --------------
 JOB             NOT NULL NUMBER
 LOG_USER        NOT NULL VARCHAR2(30)
 PRIV_USER       NOT NULL VARCHAR2(30)
 SCHEMA_USER     NOT NULL VARCHAR2(30)
 LAST_DATE                DATE
 LAST_SEC                 VARCHAR2(8)
 THIS_DATE                DATE
 THIS_SEC                 VARCHAR2(8)
 NEXT_DATE       NOT NULL DATE
 NEXT_SEC                 VARCHAR2(8)
 TOTAL_TIME               NUMBER
 BROKEN                   VARCHAR2(1)
 INTERVAL        NOT NULL VARCHAR2(200)
 FAILURES                 NUMBER
 WHAT                     VARCHAR2(4000)
 NLS_ENV                  VARCHAR2(4000)
 MISC_ENV                 RAW(32)
 INSTANCE                 NUMBER
```

Note that only the user that created the job can change it, unless he is a SYSDBA level administrator, in which case he can use the *dbms_ijob* package. This means that if different groups of replicated tables were created with separate users, then the monitoring schema will need SYSDBA privileges and *dbms_ijob* should be used instead. Otherwise, monitoring will have to run within the job scheduler of each schema. The primary data fields in *dba_jobs* are:

- BROKEN – A Boolean value that indicates if the job is active or broken (inactive).

- FAILURES – Indicates the number of failures that have been recorded for the job.

- INTERVAL – This is the interval that will occur between job executions.

- NEXT_DATE – This is the next time the job will be executed.

- SCHEMA_USER – Indicates the user that the scheduler will use to execute the job.

- WHAT – This column describes the job. This is the actual procedure that will be executed.

Broken Jobs

When the NEXT_DATE of a job arrives, the job coordinator process will assign an available background jobs process to execute the commands in the WHAT column. For replication, that is normally a refresh of a table or refresh group. Once the job has completed execution, the LAST_DATE and LAST_SEC columns are updated and the NEXT_DATE column is updated to the next execution time.

If the job process fails to execute the job (say the master database is not available) it will increment the FAILURES column and the job will be rescheduled. The retry increment starts at 1 minute, and doubles after each subsequent failure.

In the example presented here, after the first failure, the job will be rescheduled to retry after one minute. If it fails again, the FAILURES field will be incremented and the job will be re-executed after 2 minutes, then after four minutes, then eight minutes, until the FAILURES field reaches 16. Once FAILURES equals 16, the database will mark the job as broken and will not attempt execution again.

Note that a job will not wait more than the interval time before reattempting to execute the job again after a failure. So if the interval is set to 1 minute, the job will reattempt to execute every minute until 16 failures are recorded and it is marked broken. Also, the NEXT_DATE and NEXT_SEC columns are not updated until the job successfully executes, so there will never be more than one process attempting to execute a job at the same time. Since the database will automatically attempt to retry jobs with failures greater than zero but not broken, focus can be given to monitoring the broken jobs. The BROKEN column is a Boolean value set to "N" or "Y".

```
Select job
from user_jobs
where broken != 'N';
```

Knowing how to find the broken jobs and fix them makes it a simple matter to automate the process. The SQL script below will find all the broken jobs for a user, create another script to fix the broken jobs (*run_unbroken.sql*), and then run the repair script.

🖫 unbroken.sql

```
set pages 0;
set feedback off;

spool /tmp/run_unbroken.sql

select
    'exec dbms_job.broken('||
    job||
    ',FALSE,sysdate + 1/288);'
from
    user_jobs
where
    broken != 'N';

select
    'execute dbms_job.run(' ||
    job||
    ');'
from
    user_jobs
where
    broken != 'N';

spool off
set feedback on

@@/tmp/run_unbroken.sql
```

Here is an example of what the content in the generated script might look like:

```
exec dbms_job.broken(3,FALSE,sysdate + 1/288);
exec dbms_job.broken(9,FALSE,sysdate + 1/288);
exec dbms_job.broken(22,FALSE,sysdate + 1/288);
exec dbms_job.broken(23,FALSE,sysdate + 1/288);
exec dbms_job.broken(109,FALSE,sysdate + 1/288);
execute dbms_job.run(3);
```

```
execute dbms_job.run(9);
execute dbms_job.run(22);
execute dbms_job.run(23);
execute dbms_job.run(109);
```

Unix cron or the Windows Scheduler can be used to run this script on a schedule. If there are broken jobs, it will attempt to repair them. One solution is to incorporate this check in a Korn Shell script that will also send an email message if a job is still broken, so that it can be fixed manually. This script will also restart the replication if the master site is unavailable and the replication refresh jobs break. Once the master site is available, simply execute the script to unbreak each refresh job and restart the replication.

"Stalled" Jobs

Broken jobs are easy to find and repair. However, there is another problem with *dbms_jobs* that is harder to deal with. This problem is stalled or hung jobs. A stalled or hung job is an Oracle background jobs process that has stopped, but did not die or record a failure.

The stalled process may or may not be holding a lock on a replicated table. Stalled jobs are rare, but a replicated database with 180 replicated tables refreshing at intervals between 1 and 3 minutes, 24 hours a day, will eventually have a stalled process.

When a user process hangs, the user normally exits, and the database recovers resources as needed. When a background process hangs, there is no user to log off and the database will not detect that the process has stopped. The database will not recover the process resources because it has no indication that the process is in trouble. Someone must kill the stalled process.

A hung process usually cannot be killed from within the Oracle database because it is not responding. As long as the process remains, the job will not complete the refresh and replication of those tables the job supports. In order to remove the process, it must be killed at the operating system level. Once killed by the OS, all locks are recovered by the database and the unfinished refresh will be re-executed by another process. The Oracle database will also respawn the background process once it has determined that it is no longer there.

Detecting a stalled jobs process is relatively easy. Simply query the *dba_jobs* view for jobs that are falling behind the Next_Date.

```
SELECT  job, last_date,  last_sec,  broken
FROM
  dba_jobs WHERE last_date <= SYSDATE - 1/24
  AND   job != 310;
```

This query will give a list of jobs that have fallen behind by at least 1 hour. Job 310 is a purge job and it only executes every 6 hours, so it is excluded from the results.

To check for a stalled job, query the view *dba_jobs_running*. This will be helpful in discovering jobs that are falling behind and are probably stalled. (Note there is no *user_jobs_running* view.) The user that runs the script must be granted the rights to select the view *sys.dba_jobs_running*:

```
SELECT  /*+ RULE */
  b.job,  b.last_date,  b.last_sec,
  b.sid,  p.spid OSPID
FROM
  dba_jobs_running b,
  v$session s,
  v$process p
WHERE b.sid = s.sid
AND s.paddr = p.addr
;
```

> 🔔 Note the RULE hint. Without this hint the query can take a substantial amount of time to execute. This hint is needed on 9i and 10g.

This query selects jobs that are running from *dba_jobs_running*. It uses the SID of the running process and the process memory address to join to the *v$session* and *v$process* views to extract the operating system process id. Here are sample results from the execution of this script:

```
   JOB LAST_DATE   LAST_SEC          SID OSPID
---------- ---------- --------- ---------- -----
   190 09/04/2003 12:15:17         46 441
   309 09/04/2003 12:19:23         50 451
```

The results show that job 190 is being executed by session ID number 46, which is the OS process 441. If no rows are returned by this query, then there are no jobs executing at the time. The good news is that a stalled job will remain in the *dba_jobs_running* view. It is possible to extract only the stalled jobs by adding some restrictions to the query. Here is an updated query that reflects these changes:

💾 bad_jobs.sql

```
spool /tmp/bad_jobs.txt

SELECT  b.job,  b.last_date,  b.last_sec,
  b.sid,  p.spid OSPID
```

```
   v$session s,
   v$process p
WHERE b.sid = s.sid
AND s.paddr = p.addr
AND last_date <= SYSDATE - 1/24
AND    job != 310;

spool off
```

The above script will create a text file that can be emailed to an administrator, or it could be used to automatically kill the OS process. The following script may also be useful:

```
cat /tmp/bad_job.txt|grep -v "-"|grep -v JOB| \
  awk '{ print $5}'|xargs kill -9
```

This script takes the easy-to-read query results and extracts the OS process id. It then kills them from the OS. Before automating the process "execution," manually check and fix each stalled process in case there is a database problem that is causing the process to stall. This will also kill a jobs process that is waiting behind a lock.

Now that background job process problems have been covered, it is time to move on to the deferred error queue.

Monitoring the Deferred Error Queue

The second step in monitoring replication is to insure that the error queue is clear. UMVs replicate by first pushing updates back to the Master site and then pulling changes from the Master site. Both databases use the *deferred transaction queue* to pass changes across the database links.

If the UMV cannot contact the master table to push changed data, the changes will remain in the local deferred transaction queue until communication resumes. Once contact with the master site is restored, all the changes will be pushed to the master site deferred transaction queue. Once the changes have arrived in the transaction queue they are applied to the appropriate tables.

Changes that cannot be applied are placed in the *deferred error queue*. In the case where communication cannot be established between the UMV and the master table, the UMV has committed a change that has not yet propagated to the base table. Consequently it is in the error queue. Once an error for a replicated object is in the error queue, all subsequent changes will also be logged as errors. This insures that data integrity is maintained. The result would be that both the master and replicated tables continue to function, but replication has halted.

There are a number of reasons why replication might fail and the error queue might start filling. These include:

- Loss of the database link.

- Network failure.

- Some architectural change to the Mview or to the master table.

- Failed database upgrade or migration.

- The Mview Log has been lost.

- Data Conflict

The solution is to empty the error queue by fixing the error, reapplying the changes, and deleting those errors that contain no data. Data conflicts and conflict resolution are covered in detail in Chapter 7, *Conflict Resolution*. The view *deferror* provides a look into the deferred error queue. Here is its definition:

```
SQL> desc deferror

Name                 Null?     Type
------------------   --------  --------------
DEFERRED_TRAN_ID     NOT NULL  VARCHAR2(22)
ORIGIN_TRAN_DB                 VARCHAR2(128)
ORIGIN_TRAN_ID                 VARCHAR2(22)
CALLNO                         NUMBER
DESTINATION                    VARCHAR2(128)
START_TIME                     DATE
ERROR_NUMBER                   NUMBER
ERROR_MSG                      VARCHAR2(2000)
RECEIVER                       VARCHAR2(30)
```

Note that the *deferror* view is only available to privileged accounts (with the SYSDBA grant). For other user accounts to be able to see *deferror*, the GRANT command should be used to allow select authority, as seen in this example:

```
GRANT SELECT ON deferror TO pubs;
```

When an error occurs in replication using UMVs, the deferred error queue on the master site will normally contain the errors, since this is the most likely place that the error will occur. To attempt to reapply the transaction in the error queue use *dbms_defer_sys.execute_error*.

```
begin
  dbms_defer_sys.execute_error(destination=>
    'destination',deferred_tran_id=>
    'deferred_tran_id');
end;
```

Again, this can be incorporated into a script that periodically re-executes errors in the deferred error queue.

```
set pages 0 line 132 feedback off
spool /tmp/retry.sql

select
  'execute dbms_defer_sys.execute_error(destination=>'''||
    destination||''', deferred_tran_id=>'''||
    deferred_tran_id||''');'
from
  deferror;

spool off
set feedback on
spool /tmp/retry.log

@@/tmp/retry.sql

spool off
exit
```

This script is an example of dynamic SQL. It is run while logged onto the master site as the REPADMIN user. Using the DESTINATION and DEFERRED_TRAN_ID columns in *deferror*, it creates another script that is a list of commands to re-execute the errors. It then dynamically runs the scripts.

Any error that contains data will apply those changes and be removed from the error queue. Errors that contain no data will fail and remain in the error queue.

 This script is used to explain interacting with the *deferror* queue. It is a BAD idea to automatically delete errors from the error queue. Normally an error indicated that some transaction did not get applied. It is prudent to determine why the error was not applied before deleting the transaction. Automatically deleting errors from the error queue will lead to data divergence between the replicated databases.

The next step is to delete the errors that contained no data from the queue. Using the same basic script as above, execute the *dbms_defer_sys.delete_error* procedure. To delete the errors, the only thing needed is the *deferred_tran_id*, setting the destination parameter to null. The following script demonstrates this activity:

```
set pages 0 line 132 feedback off

spool /tmp/delete_error.sql
```

```
select
 'execute dbms_defer_sys.delete_error( /
  destination=>NULL,
  deferred_tran_id=>'''||deferred_tran_id||''');'
from
  deferror;

spool off
set feedback on
spool /tmp/delete_error.log

@@/tmp/delete_error.sql

spool off
exit
```

The end result of this script is the removal of all the errors remaining in the *deferror* queue. By combining the two scripts above, the errors can be re-executed with data and then the remaining errors can be deleted. The following *replication_check.ksh* Korn Shell script does exactly that. It also fixes broken and stalled jobs. Finally, it checks to see that all replication jobs are running and emails an alert if there is a problem.

🖫 replication_check.ksh

```
--
--    Copyright © 2003 by Rampant TechPress Inc.
--
--    Free for non-commercial use.
--    For commercial licensing, e-mail info@rampant.cc
--
-- ************************************************

#!/usr/bin/ksh
#
# set the directory as needed
cd /u01/oracle/sql/bei
#
# Set all the database parameters
ORACLE_SID=$1
export ORACLE_SID
ORACLE_HOME=`cat /var/opt/oracle/oratab|grep /
  $ORACLE_SID:|cut -f2 -d':'`
export ORACLE_HOME
PATH=$ORACLE_HOME/bin:$PATH
export PATH
#
# Try to reexecute errors in the defered queue then
# delete them.
$ORACLE_HOME/bin/sqlplus repadmin/passwd@navdb /
  @clear_error.sql
```

```
$ORACLE_HOME/bin/sqlplus snapadmin/snapadmin@web1sq /
  @unbroken_mm.sql

# Verify that all jobs are fixed correctly
$ORACLE_HOME/bin/sqlplus system/systemweb@web1sq /
  @bad_jobs.sql

# Email the bad jobs if there are any.
echo lines are `cat /tmp/bad_job.lst|wc -l`
# Mail the report
  newm=`cat /tmp/bad_job.lst|wc -l`
  echo $mewm
  chgflg=`expr $newm`
  if [ $chgflg -gt 3 ]
  then
    cat /tmp/bad_job.lst|mailx -s "Subject: /
          Bad Jobs on MYDB" john@mydesk.com
```

Restarting Replication after an Extended Shutdown of the Master Site

When the master site is shutdown for any reason, replication jobs will start breaking. Once the master site is restarted, replication to the master site will need to be restarted. Use the *replication_check.ksh* script to automatically restart replication on the UMV site after an extended outage of the master site. Since all the replicated tables will begin refreshing one at a time, it may take awhile for the UMV to complete. Experience has shown that it is more efficient to allow the *replication_check.ksh* to restart the UMV replication than to manually try and restart all the jobs.

The *replication_check.ksh* script executes on the set schedule, but if waiting for the next execution is not an option, the script can be executed manually. The jobs can also be restarted using Oracle Enterprise Manager. However, each job must be restarted.

Monitoring the Mview Log

The Mview log can sometimes grow unconstrained. This usually occurs when a remote database with a refreshing Mview is removed without first dropping the Mview. Thus, the master site will continue to collect data in an effort to update the remote Mview.

If Mview logs are growing rapidly, rows may need to be purged from the Mview log. This is done via the *dbms_mview.purge_log* procedure. Use this procedure carefully so as to not be forced to perform full refreshes of remote Mviews.

You can keep track of the growth of the Mview log via the *dba_extents* view, with a little help from the *dba_mview_logs* view. The following script can be used to keep track of the growth of Mview logs:

```
SELECT a.log_owner, a.log_table, sum(b.bytes), count(*)
FROM dba_mview_logs a, dba_extents b
WHERE a.log_owner=b.owner
AND a.log_table=b.segment_name
GROUP by a.log_owner, a.log_table;
```

Here is some sample output:

```
LOG_OWNER   LOG_TABLE                         SUM(B.BYTES)   COUNT(*)
----------  ----------------------------      ------------   ---------
PUBS        MLOG$_BOOK                               65536           1
PUBS        MLOG$_SALES                              65536           1
PUBS        MLOG$_STORE                              65536           1
EMP_USER    MLOG$_EMPLOYEE                           65536           1
```

In this case, there are four Mview logs. Each is 65k, a manageable size, and each is one extent.

The important point here is that if the Mview logs become very large, performance of refreshes can suffer because Oracle has to scan the Mview log table in order to perform Mview refreshes.

 Before removing a database, always make sure that all Mviews are dropped from that database.

Conclusion

Replication is a complicated process that must be monitored continuously to insure data is successfully propagating between sites. The DBA can either manually monitor the parameters or establish scripts that will watch for problems, repair them if possible, and provide notification when intervention is required.

Focus attention on monitoring those key situations that will cause replication to fail.

- Broken Jobs

- Stalled Jobs

- Deferred Error Queue

As the replication environment grows, other areas unique to the specific system will require monitoring.

Multi-Master
Replication

In this chapter, the most powerful type of replication that Oracle offers will be explored, Multi-Master replication (MMR). Features of MMR will be examined and what it can offer before mapping the steps involved in planning MMR replication. An example of MMR replication in action is included. Finally, various MMR maintenance issues to be aware of will be covered.

An Introduction to Multi-Master Replication

How to create and use read-only and updatable materialized views has been covered previously. They offer the powerful ability to replicate data in tables across separate databases. With multi-master replication, more than just database tables can be replicated. The following can also be replicated:

- Tables

- Indexes

- Procedures, functions, and triggers

- Packages

- User-defined types (Oracle9i)

As always, there are plusses and minuses to using multi-master replication. The positive benefits of MMR include the following:

- Replicates more objects, including user-defined objects.

- Updates or modifies the objects being replicated. Adding a column to a table at the master definition site can be replicated to other master sites.

- Replicates with any number of other databases. Any master site can replicate with other master sites, updatable Mview sites, and read-only Mview sites.

However, there are some downsides such as:

- Potentially large network bandwidth requirements - Not only does multi-master push and pull changes between sites, it also sends acknowledgements and quite a bit of administrative data.

- Reduced Performance - Complexity and robustness comes at a price. MMR involves the use of triggers and procedures. This can result in a database performance hit. Depending on how much data that is being replicated, this performance hit can be substantial.

- Significant increases in administration requirements - When problems appear in the database, the DBA must insure that replication is not the cause or that the cause is not replicated to other databases. Database performance tuning and problem resolution become more complicated by an order of magnitude.

- Database changes require additional planning - Rolling out a new version of an application can be much more difficult. Each new version will require revisiting the design of replication.

The considerations above should reinforce the earlier recommendation not to implement a higher level of replication than needed.

Multi-master replication is powerful. It is also complicated to create and monitor the replication environment. Because of this complexity, multi-master replication requires some additional planning.

Planning Multi-Master Replication

There are a number of considerations when planning an MMR site. First, decide what needs to be replicated. Then, configure the tables for replication.

Begin preparing by deciding what data needs to be replicated. Because of the bandwidth requirements to support multi-master replication, only replicate those objects that are required at the remote sites. Again, only use MMR on those objects that require MMR.

A master definition site can contain any number of master groups. The reason for grouping replication objects is to insure data integrity. If different objects replicate to different master sites, they should be placed in separate groups. Unlike updatable Mviews, every object in a master group will replicate to all other master sites that support that group.

Configuring Tables for Replication

Before replicating tables with MMR, make sure the table's logical design will support MMR.

Consider the following configuration issues:

- Establishing primary keys

- Establishing foreign keys

- Establishing database parameters

- Validating that the replication packages are installed

- Creating replication administration accounts

- Creating database links

- Creating push and purge jobs

Configuring Primary Keys

To replicate tables, the database must identify rows uniquely. This is normally accomplished by using primary keys. If a table does not have a primary key defined, one can be defined by using a column or set of columns to uniquely identify rows. The process of defining a row or set of row essentially defines a primary key on that table. It is recommended that primary keys be defined on all tables used for replication to avoid confusion.

Using Sequences to Create Primary Keys

If a table simply has no row or group of rows that uniquely identifies it, a sequence will have to be utilized to establish the primary key. The sequence creates a special type of primary key known as a pseudo key or surrogate key.

Using sequences as primary keys introduces a data integrity problem as multiple sites add rows to the table. If every site starts the sequence at 1, the first row will contain a key of "1." When another site adds a row it will also assign a key of "1." This will create a key conflict that must be remedied.

There are two easy ways to avoid this conflict. One is to have each master site begin the sequence at a different number. For example, Site 1 starts at 1, Site 2 starts at 100,000, and Site 3 starts at 200,000. For the first 99,999 rows inserted at one site this plan works. However, the 100,000th row from any site will create a key conflict.

Another method is for each site to start all the sequences at 1, but to concatenate the site name to the key. Site NAVDB would thus insert rows with the primary key being NAVDB1, NAVDB2, and so forth. The MYDB site would use MYDB1, MYDB2, and so forth. This method provides a more flexible solution, especially if additional master sites may be added at a later date. Conflict resolution is covered in greater detail in Chapter 7, *Conflict Resolution*.

A table with a primary key defined will have a primary key index that the database uses to enforce the constraint. This index may be defined by the user or created by the database. When the table is added to the replication group, the primary key index

---

does not have to be included. When the table is replicated to another master site, the remote site will automatically build the primary key index.

Foreign Keys

Foreign keys are used to enforce referential integrity. Normally, an index is created on the foreign key column of the child table to keep from having to execute a full table scan on the child table every time the parent table is updated. By adding the foreign key index to the master replication group, the child table does not have to be replicated and referential integrity can still be enforced. An update to the child table will update the foreign key index, which is replicated to the remote sites. However, if a child table is replicated, the parent table must also be replicated to maintain the integrity.

Database Parameters

The only difference in parameter values when implementing multi-master replication over updatable materialized replication is to add an additional 80M to the shared pool size on all master sites. Below is a quick synopsis of *init.ora* changes to support multi-master replication.

PARAMETER NAME	DEFAULT VALUE	RECOMMENDED VALUE
compatible	Depends on the version of Oracle you are using.	Set compatible to the version of Oracle that you are using in order to use all replication features of that version of the database
db_domain	.WORLD	This is the extension component of the local databases Global Name. If not defined, it will default to ".WORLD"
distributed_ transactions	.25 * the parameter setting for transactions	Add 5 + 2 per master to the existing value. Note this is obsolete in Oracle9i and later.
global_names	FALSE	global_names must be set to TRUE in each database that will be involved in advanced replication.
job_queue_ processes	0	This parameter must be set to a value of at least one. Higher values will allow more parallel replication of objects. We recommend 3 + 1 per additional master.
open_links	4	open_links defines the number of concurrent database links that are required for a given database. This parameter needs to be configured for an initial setting of 4 + 2 additional links for each master site.

PARAMETER NAME	DEFAULT VALUE	RECOMMENDED VALUE
parallel_automatic_ tuning	FALSE	Oracle9i offers this parameter to help establish the correct level of parallelism. Set it to TRUE to allow Oracle to determine the best configuration for parallel operations.
parallel_max_ servers	Derived based on the parameters: cpu_count, parallel_ automatic_tuning, parallel_ adaptive_multi_ user	Only important if you need parallel propagation, which is recommended. You should configure this parameter's value high enough to allow sufficient parallel servers to be started. Generally, the default is sufficient.
parallel_min_ servers	0	Set this value to the number of parallel streams that you are expecting. We suggest 2.
processes	Derived from the value of the parameter parallel_max_ servers	Add at least 12 to the current value.
replication_ dependency_ tracking	TRUE	Should be set to the default value.
shared_pool_size	OS Dependent	Add at least 80m to the shared pool for most MMR replication instillations.

Table 6.1: *init.ora Changes to Support Multi-master Replication*

Verify the Replication Packages Are Loaded

As with all forms of advanced replication, the replication packages must be valid. Ask SYS or SYSTEM to execute the following query to identify invalid objects in the database.

```
SELECT count(*)
FROM   dba_objects
WHERE status = 'INVALID'
AND owner IN ('SYS', 'SYSTEM');
```

For additional information concerning installing and verifying the replication packages, refer to Chapter 2, *Preparing to Use Replication*.

Remember that the user REPADMIN administers each master site. When conducting maintenance or other administration tasks, the DBA must make sure to work on the correct database site.

Creating the User Repadmin

Just as with updatable Mviews, the replication administrator is a user called REPADMIN. The REPADMIN user is created in the same way and granted the same privileges on all master sites. Passwords can be different at each site for additional security.

```
create user repadmin identified by repadmin;
grant connect, resource to repadmin;
execute dbms_repcat_admin.grant_admin_any_schema('repadmin');
grant comment any table to repadmin;
grant lock any table to repadmin;
execute dbms_defer_sys.register_propagator('repadmin');
```

Normally, REPADMIN is the administrator, receiver, and the propagator. These are three distinct functions:

- The administrator maintains the master group, adds, or removes objects, etc.

- The propagator is responsible for pushing items in the deferred transaction queue to all other master sites.

- The receiver takes items that have arrived in the deferred transaction queue and applies them to the local objects.

Oracle recommends (and these authors agree!) that REPADMIN be used to perform all three tasks when establishing the replication environment. For additional security, a separate user can be established as the receiver and propagator, similar to the way REPPROXY was used in Chapter 4, *Updatable Materialized Views*. When separate users are utilized to perform these tasks, either the trusted or untrusted security model will be implemented.

Trusted and Untrusted Security Models

If a separate user is created as the propagator and/or the receiver, the trusted or untrusted security model can be implemented. The trusted model allows the propagator/receiver to support all master groups on all systems. The untrusted model assigns specific groups to a receiver and the receiver only has access to those specific groups. Regardless of the model choosen, there are a few rules that can not be violated:

- A master site can have only one propagator.

- A propagator has the "execute any procedure" grant.

- A master site can have multiple receivers.

- A master group can have only one receiver per master site.

- A receiver is not granted "execute any procedure".

There are three main options for establishing our replication admin users:

- The REPADMIN does it all approach

- The trusted model

- The untrusted model

Each of these are covered in a bit more detail next.

Repadmin Does All - The recommended approach

Most multi-master replication uses one admin user, REPADMIN, who acts as administrator, propagator, and receiver. Since REPADMIN is a propagator, it has the "execute any procedure" grant, and therefore has access to any procedure in the database, regardless of whether it is part of replication. REPADMIN is on every master site with these privileges and has access to all replication groups, objects, and procedures.

Trusted Model - Separate User for each Task

In the trusted model, there are three users that each performs a separate task. REPADMIN administers the replication, but since he is not a propagator, he is not granted "execute any procedure." Another user, for this example will be referred to as REPPROP, is the propagator. This user has the "execute any procedure" privilege only on his master site, and he has no access to anything on other master sites. A third user, called REPRECV for example, is defined as the receiver for only that master site. REPRECV is the receiver for all master groups on that master site. This model works well when all master groups are propagated to all master sites. There is no reason to define multiple receivers since they will each have access to all master groups on the site.

Untrusted Model - Separate User for each Task, Multiple Receivers

The difference between the trusted and untrusted model is that in the untrusted model all master groups are not replicated to all master sites. Since there is only one propagator per master site, and he will try to replicate all the master groups to all the master sites, it is the receiver who determines which master groups are applied at each master site.

In Figure 6.1 the master definition site has three master groups. REP_GROUP1 replicates with master sites A and C. REP_GROUP2 replicates with master sites A, C, and D. This configuration can use a single administrator so REPADMIN can perform all the tasks on the master definition site and on master site A. But master sites B, C, and D must implement the untrusted model to limit the master groups each site replicates.

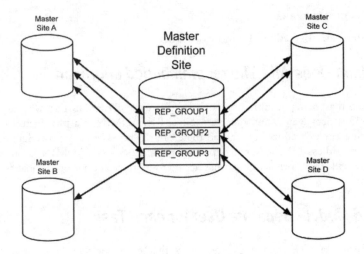

Figure 6.1: *Untrusted Security Model*

Master site B will implement a receiver that only receives REP_GROUP3. Master site C will implement a receiver that only receives REP_GROUP1 and REP_GROUP2. Master site D will implement a receiver that only receives REP_GROUP2 and REP_GROUP3.

Add multiple master definition sites and it becomes apparent how multi-master replication can become quite complicated. One significant advantage of both the trusted and untrusted models is that no user has the *"execute any procedure"* grant on a remote site. All three users only have grants to their own master site.

Creating the Trusted and Untrusted Models

The following is an example of a trusted model. Here is the SQL used to create the different user accounts. This SQL will be executed on all master sites:

```
connect system/?????

create user repadmin identified by repadmin;
grant connect, resource to repadmin;
grant grant execute any procedure to repadmin;
execute dbms_repcat_admin.grant_admin_any_schema(
        'repadmin');
grant comment any table to repadmin;
grant lock any table to repadmin;
```

```
create user repprop identified by repprop;
grant connect, resource to repprop;
grant grant execute any procedure to repaprop;
execute dbms_defer_sys.register_propagator(
          'repprop');

create user reprecv identified by reprecv;
grant connect, resource to reprecv;
grant grant execute any procedure to reprecy;
execute dbms_repcat_admin.register_user_repgroup( username =>
'reprecv',    privilege_type  => 'receiver',    list_of_gnames =>
NULL);
```

The three users were created, each having separate tasks, and none having access to remote sites.

To implement the untrusted model, create REPADMIN and REPPROP, just as in the previous example. Then create two master groups and the receiver. The master group must exist before making a user a receiver. In this example, user REPRECV is registered as a receiver for the master groups REP_GROUP2 and REP_GROUP3.

```
connect system/?????

create user repadmin identified by repadmin;
grant connect, resource to repadmin;
execute dbms_repcat_admin.grant_admin_any_schema(
          'repadmin');
grant comment any table to repadmin;
grant lock any table to repadmin;

create user repprop identified by repprop;
grant connect, resource to repprop;
execute dbms_defer_sys.register_propagator(
          'repprop');

create user reprecv identified by reprecv;
grant connect, resource to reprecv;

-- First create the groups.
execute dbms_repcat.create_master_repgroup(
          gname=> 'REP_GROUP2');

execute dbms_repcat.create_master_repgroup(
          gname=> 'REP_GROUP3');

-- Now register the reciever.
execute dbms_repcat_admin.register_user_repgroup(
  username => 'reprecv',
  privilege_type  => 'receiver',
  list_of_gnames => 'REP_GROUP2, REP_GROUP3');
```

Finally, it's time to deal with the user who owns the data being replicated. In this example, the PUBS schema is going to be replicated from the NAVDB.WORLD to

---

the PUBS schema in MYDB.WORLD. The PUBS schema on the remote sites will start out empty. No special grants are required for the schema owner.

> 🖫 **The script can be accessed from the online code depot.**

Creating Database Links

The next step in preparing for multi-master replication is establishing the database links. Links must be established in both directions between master sites. Database links are covered in Chapter 2, *Preparing To Use Replication*. Here, two private links are going to be created between the two REPADMIN users.

```
connect repadmin/repadmin@navdb.world

create database link MYDB.WORLD
  connect to repadmin identified by repadmin
  using 'MYDB.WORLD';

connect repadmin/repadmin@mydb.world

create private database link NAVDB.WORLD
  connect to repadmin identified by repadmin
  using 'NAVDB.WORLD';
```

If there are other master sites in the replication setup, create links in both directions to all other master sites. Note that this is different from the previous forms of replication with materialized views. Since MMR is a two-way form of replication, there need to be database links going in both directions.

For either the trusted or untrusted model, the database links must be created from the local propagator to the registered receiver at the remote site. REPADMIN does not need a database link if he is not acting as a propagator or receiver. Here, the database links are being created to support the examples later in this book:

```
connect repprop/repprop@navdb.world

create database link MYDB.WORLD
  connect to reprecv identified by reprecv
  using 'MYDB.WORLD';

connect repprop/repprop@mydb.world

create database link NAVDB.WORLD
  connect to reprecv identified by reprecv
  using 'NAVDB.WORLD';
```

Each master site only needs to be linked with one paired master site, though from a HA redundancy point of view this may be desirable. Each master site does not need to be linked to all other master sites.

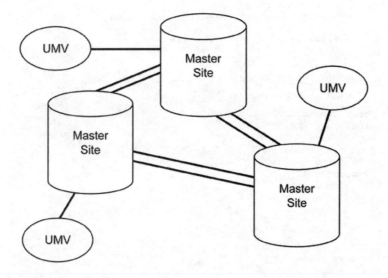

Figure 6.2: *Linking Master Sites*

Database links can also be created in Oracle Enterprise Manager. Please refer to Chapter 2, *Preparing To Use Replication*, for additional details.

Creating Push/Purge Jobs

All changes to replication objects are applied at the local site and placed in the deferred transaction queue. A job is needed to periodically push those changes to other master sites. A job is also needed to remove the changes from the transaction queue after they have been pushed.

These two tasks are split into two jobs to increase efficiency. The push needs to happen as quickly and efficiently as possible. The purge needs to happen often enough to keep the queue manageable. The push/purge jobs are created using the *schedule_push* and *schedule_purge* procedures in the Oracle supplied *dbms_defer_sys* package. The schedule will be to every minute and purge every hour. Purge more often when dealing with a system that has a high transaction rate.

📰 **MM_PushPurge.sql**

```
--    Free for non-commercial use.
--    For commercial licensing, e-mail info@rampant.cc
--
-- *********************************************

-- Add jobs to NAVDB
connect repadmin/repadmin@navdb

begin
  dbms_defer_sys.schedule_push(
    destination => 'MYDB.WORLD',
    interval => 'SYSDATE + 1/(60*24)',
    next_date => sysdate,
    stop_on_error => FALSE,
    delay_seconds => 0,
    parallelism => 1);
end;
/

begin
dbms_defer_sys.schedule_purge(
  next_date => sysdate,
  interval => 'sysdate + 1/24',
  delay_seconds => 0,
  rollback_segment => '');
end;
/

-- Add jobs to MYDB
connect repadmin/repadmin@mydb

begin
  dbms_defer_sys.schedule_push(
    destination => 'NAVDB.WORLD',
    interval => 'SYSDATE + 1/(60*24)',
    next_date => sysdate,
    stop_on_error => FALSE,
    delay_seconds => 0,
    parallelism => 1);
end;
/

begin
dbms_defer_sys.schedule_purge(
  next_date => sysdate,
  interval => 'sysdate + 1/24',
  delay_seconds => 0,
  rollback_segment => '');
end;
```

Although there is no way to create purge/push jobs in OEM, they can be edited there. Under the Distribution → Advanced Replication → Schedule tabs, both the push and purge jobs can be found. Modify them by selecting the edit button or changing the parameters and selecting apply. Below, the push job was changed to execute every 10 seconds.

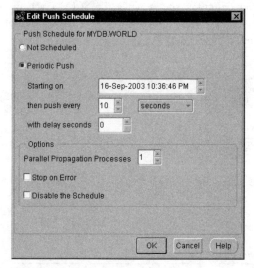

Figure 6.3: *OEM Edit Push Job*

Now that want needs to be replicated has been identified, it is time to create the Master Definition Site on NAVDB.WORLD and then replicate it on MYDB.WORLD. This can be done using the command line or with Oracle Enterprise Manager.

Setting Up MMR – By Example

In this section, an example will be used to demonstrate how to set up MMR. The Master Definition Site will be explained briefly before creating the master replication group.

The Master Definition Site

The master definition site is the "home base" for a master group. It contains the base objects that are replicated to the remote sites. For this example, the master definition site is NAVDB and the remote master site is MYDB.

Once created, the master definition site will automatically replicate itself to the new master site(s). There can be only one master definition site for a replicated object. All changes to a replicated object are performed at the master definition site and propagated to all other master sites.

Within a replication environment there can be multiple master definition sites as shown in Figure 6.4. For example, the PUBS schema could be replicated in master group REP_GROUP1 from master definition site A while the SCOTT schema is replicated in REP_GROUP2 from master definition site B. Both sites are master definition sites but on separate objects.

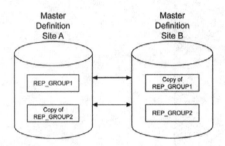

Figure 6.4: *Multiple Master Definition Sites*

Create the Master Replication Group

The master replication group contains all the objects that will be replicated. If the master group is going to also support updatable materialized views, materialized view logs must exist on those tables before adding them to the master group. This example will create a master replication group and add three tables, *author*, *book_author*, and *book*. The script *MM_MasterGroup.sql* will replicate the entire schema.

The script can be accessed from the online code depot.

🖫 MM_MasterGroup.sql

Here is an example of the creation of a master replication group called GROUP1.

```
connect repadmin/repadmin@navdb

BEGIN
   DBMS_REPCAT.CREATE_MASTER_REPGROUP(
      gname => '"GROUP1"',
      qualifier => '',
      group_comment => '');
END;
/
```

Adding Tables to the Master Replication Group

Next, it's time to add the *author* table from the PUBS schema. The *create_master_repobject* procedure of the *dbms_repcat* package is used for this, as seen in this example:

```
BEGIN
    DBMS_REPCAT.CREATE_MASTER_REPOBJECT(
        gname => '"GROUP1"',
        type => 'TABLE',
        oname => '"AUTHOR"',
        sname => '"PUBS"');
END;
/
```

Now, the remaining two tables are added.

```
BEGIN
    DBMS_REPCAT.CREATE_MASTER_REPOBJECT(
        gname => '"GROUP1"',
        type => 'TABLE',
        oname => '"BOOK"',
        sname => '"PUBS"');
END;
/
BEGIN
    DBMS_REPCAT.CREATE_MASTER_REPOBJECT(
        gname => '"GROUP1"',
        type => 'TABLE',
        oname => '"BOOK_AUTHOR"',
        sname => '"PUBS"');
END;
/
```

****

The following errors might be generated when executing the above code:

```
SQL> BEGIN
  2      DBMS_REPCAT.CREATE_MASTER_REPOBJECT(
  3          gname => '"GROUP1"',
  4          type => 'TABLE',
  5          oname => '"BOOK"',
  6          sname => '"PUBS"',
  7          use_existing_object=>TRUE);
  8   END;
  9   /
BEGIN
*
ERROR at line 1:
ORA-23309: object "PUBS"."BOOK" of type TABLE exists
ORA-06512: at "SYS.DBMS_SYS_ERROR", line 105
ORA-06512: at "SYS.DBMS_REPCAT_MAS", line 2552
```

```
ORA-06512: at "SYS.DBMS_REPCAT", line 562
ORA-06512: at line 2
```

The error message indicates that the given table has already been set up for some form of replication. This is very possible if previous examples from this book have been run. This problem can be cleared by using the *delete_master_repobject* procedure of the *dbms_repcat* supplied procedure, as seen in this example:

```
exec
dbms_repcat.drop_master_repobject('PUBS','BOOK_AUTHOR','TABLE');
```

****

Tables without Primary Keys

Suppose, in the example above, that the *book* table has a defined primary key but the other two tables do not. Oracle must be told how to uniquely identify rows in the *author* and *book_author* tables.

```
BEGIN
   DBMS_REPCAT.SET_COLUMNS(
      sname => '"PUBS"',
      oname => '"AUTHOR"',
      column_list => '"AUTHOR_KEY"');
END;
/
BEGIN
   DBMS_REPCAT.SET_COLUMNS(
      sname => '"PUBS"',
      oname => '"BOOK_AUTHOR"',
      column_list =>
       '"AUTHOR_KEY","BOOK_KEY"');
END;
/
```

> Be careful with spaces inside of parameters contained within quotes. It's easy to make a mistake, for "*author*" is not the same as "*author* ".

The *author_key* uniquely identifies the authors. Unique rows in *book_author* are determined by the two columns *author_key* and *book_key*. Essentially what this has done is defined two quasi-primary keys on those two tables. Any row that violates these keys will result in a key conflict, which must be resolved. Note this is not the same as an actual primary key. No index is created and duplicate values can be insert into the table. If at all possible, it's preferable to define the primary key on the table.

Generate Replication Support

The procedure *dbms_repcat.genrate_replication_support* will generate replication support for the three tables. This creates the objects, triggers, procedures, etc. required for Oracle to support replication. Here is an example:

```
BEGIN
    DBMS_REPCAT.GENERATE_REPLICATION_SUPPORT(
        sname => '"PUBS"',
        oname => '"AUTHOR"',
        type => 'TABLE',
        min_communication => TRUE,
        generate_80_compatible => FALSE);
END;
/
BEGIN
    DBMS_REPCAT.GENERATE_REPLICATION_SUPPORT(
        sname => '"PUBS"',
        oname => '"BOOK"',
        type => 'TABLE',
        min_communication => TRUE,
        generate_80_compatible => FALSE);
END;
/
BEGIN
    DBMS_REPCAT.GENERATE_REPLICATION_SUPPORT(
        sname => '"PUBS"',
        oname => '"BOOK_AUTHOR"',
        type => 'TABLE',
        min_communication => TRUE,
        generate_80_compatible => FALSE);
END;
/
```

Check the view *dba_repcatlog* for errors.

```
SELECT COUNT(*)
FROM dba_repcatlog;
```

This view should be empty. If not, wait until it is empty before continuing. Once any errors appearing in *dba_repcatlog* have been dealt with, start replication support.

```
BEGIN
    DBMS_REPCAT.RESUME_MASTER_ACTIVITY(
    gname => '"GROUP1"');
END;
/
```

At this point, the master definition site is ready to replicate GROUP1 to other master sites.

Adding Additional Master Sites

Once the master definition site has created and populated a master replication group, it is relatively easy to add a master site. Before adding a new master site, the steps outlined in the planning section of this chapter must be executed. The REPADMIN user must be created and have the appropriate grants and be defined as the propagator. The database links must be created and functioning, along with the push/purge jobs. Once this has been accomplished, it is time to add the new master site.

The script *MM_AddMaster.sql* will add the MYDB.WORLD site to the replication scheme. It is run from the master definition site only!

Replication support on the master definition site must be suspended whenever a master site is added.

🖫 MM_AddMaster.sql

```
--
--     Copyright © 2003 by Rampant TechPress Inc.
--
--     Free for non-commercial use.
--     For commercial licensing, e-mail info@rampant.cc
--
-- ***********************************************

connect repadmin/repadmin@navdb

BEGIN
    DBMS_REPCAT.SUSPEND_MASTER_ACTIVITY(
    gname => '"GROUP1"');
END;
```

This command will stop replication support, not only on the master definition site, but also on every other master site in the replication scheme. It also places all objects in the master group at all master sites in read-only status to maintain data integrity.

Now add the new master site.

```
BEGIN
    DBMS_REPCAT.ADD_MASTER_DATABASE(
    gname => '"GROUP1"',
master => 'MYDB.WORLD');
END;
/
```

This command will replicate all objects in GROUP1 to the MYDB.WORLD database.

To complete the process, restart replication support.

```
BEGIN
    DBMS_REPCAT.RESUME_MASTER_ACTIVITY(
    gname => '"GROUP1"');
END;
/
```

Replication activity will restart on all master sites.

Note that all activity took place on the master definition site. *dbms_recat.add_master_site* took care of creating the replicated objects in the PUBS schema on MYDB.WORLD.

Adding additional master just repeats this process:

1.   Prep the new master site

2.   Create REPADMIN user

3.   Create database links

4.   Create the push/purge jobs

5.   At the master definition site

6.   Stop replication activity

7.   Add the new master site

8.   Resume replication activity

9.   Verify and test at both sites

Adding additional master sites is even easier in OEM.

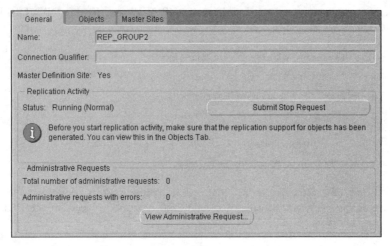

Figure 6.5: *OEM Master Group Status Page*

Log on to the master definition site (NAVDB) as REPADMIN and navigate down to REP_GROUP2. Replication activity is Running (normal), so replication activity needs to be stopped by clicking the "Submit Stop Request" button. Select the Master Sites tab at the top of the screen and select Add. This will bring up the "Add master site to the group" window as shown in Figure 6.6.

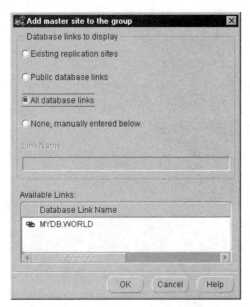

Figure 6.6: *OEM Master Group Add Master Site*

Since multi-master replication requires the use of global names, the database links to remote master sites will be names for the site. Select "All database links" to display available links. For this example, select MYDB.WORLD and click OK. The next window allows the propagation methods to be changed as shown in Figure 6.7. For this example, the defaults will be used.

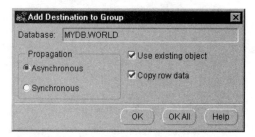

Figure 6.7: *OEM Master Group Add Destination*

If OK is selected, the selection will apply only to this master site. If OK All is selected, the selections will apply to all master sites.

Clicking Apply will cause the wizard to execute the propagation of the master group to all master sites. OEM displays a rather cryptic message "Applying User Changes..." as it propagates the master group objects. The last step is to restart the replication activity.

At this point, log onto a master site and verify that the empty PUBS schema now contains all the objects in the master group.

With multi-master replication going, it is imperative that it continues to function.

MMR and OEM

Here is a quick look at the creation of the master definition site's master replication group using OEM. The starting point is with the user REPADMIN created and the required grants executed. The push/purge jobs are in place, as are the database links.

Start Oracle Enterprise Manager (OEM), either by navigating from the Start button on Windows or by executing the Unix/Linux command:

```
oemapp console &
```

Either log on to the Management Server if one is being used or select Stand-alone.

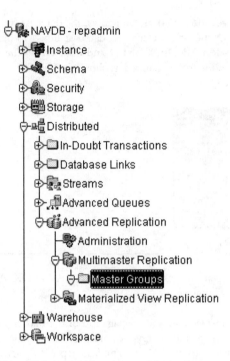

Figure 6.8: *OEM Navigation to Master Groups*

Now, log onto the database containing the data to be replicated as REPADMIN. Navigate down through the folders to Multi-Master Replication and the Master Groups as shown in Figure 6.9. Right click on the Master Groups folder and select create.

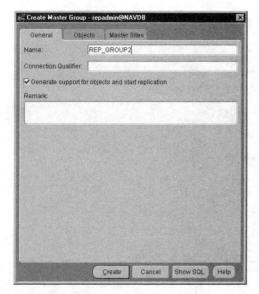

Figure 6.9: *OEM Create Master Group*

For this example, the master replication group is named REP_GROUP2. To manually generate replication support for each object, uncheck the box. The Connection Qualifier is to identify a special type of database link, such as through a modem, which must be set up prior to creating the master group.

The next step is to add objects to the group by selecting the Objects tab at the top and then selecting the Add button. This will bring up the "Add objects to group" window (Figure 6.10). Object types and schema owners can be mixed within a master group.

In this example, all the objects in the PUBS schema will be replicated. After selecting PUBS from the schema combo box, check all the boxes to display all objects in the Available Objects box. Select each object and click the Add button.

Notice that no primary key indexes were included. Each master site will automatically create primary key indexes on all replicated tables that have them defined. Clicking the OK button will cause the wizard to include the selected objects in the master group.

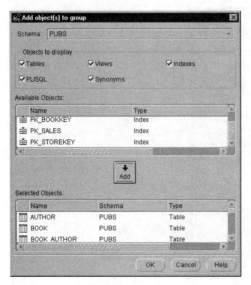

Figure 6.10: *OEM Master Group Add Objects Window*

As the wizard adds each table, it will verify that it contains a primary key. If not, the wizard will prompt the user to define a column or columns that will uniquely identify rows in the table (Figure 6.11). In this case, the *author* table does not have a primary key defined. The AUTHOR_KEY column uniquely identifies each author and can be used as a primary key. The wizard will require the identification of columns that uniquely identify rows for every table without a primary key.

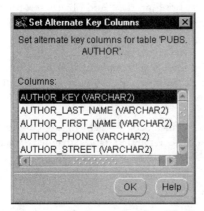

Figure 6.11: *OEM Set Alternate Key Columns*

If a table exists that does not contain unique rows because duplicate rows are allowed, then a sequence or some other method will need to be utilized to create a primary key for the table. Cancel the wizard, key the table, and then restart the process. As far as replication is concerned, primary keys are being defined on all tables being replicated. Any violation of these keys, whether defined with primary keys or with set alternate columns, will result in a key collision that must be resolved.

Once the wizard verifies each table's key, it will list them in the Objects tab (Figure 6.12). At this point, additional objects can be added or removed as required. Remote master sites can also be added to accept the replicated group.

Adding master sites is a daunting task, so added them at this time is not recommended. Suppose master sites are added and the wizard replicates the master group to each master site. If the replication fails to function, there would be no way to determine what caused the problem.

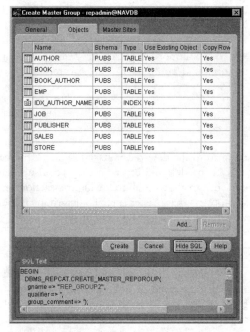

Figure 6.12: *OEM Create Master Group Objects List*

The "Show SQL" button was selected to display a list of the PL/SQL commands the wizard will use to create the master group. It is highly recommended that you copy and paste these commands into a text file. If the wizard fails, each command can be executed individually to locate the problem. Select Create to execute the commands and create the master group. OEM will indicate that it has successfully created the master group when it has finished.

Maintaining Multi-Master Replication

Replication is now set up and running. While getting it up and running is quite an accomplishment, there is still the task of keeping it running to consider. On top of that, the system has to be maintained by performing such tasks as adding and removing objects from master groups and loading and removing data. There is also the issue of re-synchronizing data after fixing problems.

Monitoring Replication

Chapter 5, *Monitoring Updatable Materialized Views,* covered methods to monitor the replication jobs and the deferred error queue. Monitoring multi-master replication is monitored in the same way (via *dba_jobs*), with the exception that each master site must be monitored.

Each master site has three jobs that support replication: *push*, *purge*, and *do_deferred_repcat_admin* jobs. Each job must continue to run for replication to function.

Deferred Error Queue

When a receiver gets a data transaction from the deferred transaction queue but can not apply it, the transaction is placed in the deferred error queue. To insure data integrity, once there is a transaction in the error queue, all following transactions end up in the error queue and replication stops on that master site. To determine if there are errors in the deferred error queue use the following SQL statement:

```
select count(*) from deferror;
```

Any returned number greater than zero indicates that there are errors in the queue. The transactions in the error queue must be applied or deleted from the queue for replication to function. Chapter 5 details the scripts to monitor and correct failed replication jobs and errors in the error queue.

Key Conflicts

There are a number of reasons that transactions end up in the error queue. One of the most common is due to key conflicts. This happens when a table with a defined primary key and a row from another master site conflicts with a row already in the table. Oracle will not allow the conflicting row to be inserted into the table.

In a normal environment, the transaction would simply rollback. In a replication environment, the row has already been applied at the originating master site, so a roll back is not possible. This transaction will end up in the error queue unless conflict resolution is defined.

Key conflicts do not just happen on primary keys. Remember when that table was added without a primary key and *set columns* was used to identify columns that uniquely identified rows? The replication support defined a key on those columns, and any transaction that violated the uniqueness of those columns was rejected. That is why using *set columns* would, for the purpose of replication, define a primary key on those columns. Conflict resolution will be further covered in Chapter 7.

Adding and Removing Objects

Adding and removing objects is easy, provided they are not large. Simply stop replication activity. Add the object to the master group at the master definition site and restart replication. The new object will be propagated to all master sites in the replication environment.

```
connect repadmin/repadmin@navdb

BEGIN
    DBMS_REPCAT.SUSPEND_MASTER_ACTIVITY(
    gname => '"GROUP1"');
END;
/

BEGIN
    DBMS_REPCAT.CREATE_MASTER_REPOBJECT(
      gname => '"GROUP1"',
      type => 'TABLE',
      oname => '"CUSTOMER"',
      sname => '"PUBS"',
      copy_rows => TRUE,
      use_existing_object => TRUE);
END;
/

BEGIN
    DBMS_REPCAT.RESUME_MASTER_ACTIVITY(
    gname => '"GROUP1"');
END;/
```

In the code above, the *customer* table was added to the master replication group. When replication activity is resumed, the *customer* table will be replicated to all other master sites. But what if the table contains 5 million rows of data? It may take days to propagate the table to the remote sites. In this case, one of the methods shown below should be used.

Moving Large Data Sets

Replication propagates data one change at a time. If 300 rows are inserted into a replicated table, those 300 rows are propagated and applied one row at a time to insure data integrity.

Oracle supports parallel propagation across the database links, but the rows must be inserted at each master site in order. This is not a problem for even relatively high transaction rates on OLTP systems. However, if a million rows of data are added, it could take hours or days to propagate. And if that were not bad enough, the table that the data was loaded into will be read-only until the propagation is completed.

Another example is in the replication of the PUBS schema. If that schema contained millions of rows of data, the replication creation could take days. There must be a better way to load data into a replicated table. There is, and it is called offline instantiation.

Offline Instantiation

Offline instantiation allows the master group object to be created on the remote sites and then replication is placed on top of those objects. While this method can greatly speed up the creation or loading of replication objects, it is not without its own issues. The base objects must be read-only from the time the data begins moving until replication can assume control. If the base tables are updated, then the copy will not be in sync.

Although the mechanics of offline instantiation are simple, the execution is not. Basically, the master group is created with false "copy_rows." This tells the master group to use the rows already at the remote site. No data checks are performed. If the tables are not in sync, then they will begin replication out of sync and stay that way.

```
BEGIN
   DBMS_REPCAT.CREATE_MASTER_REPOBJECT(
      gname => '"GROUP1"',
      type => 'TABLE',
      oname => '"BOOK"',
      sname => '"PUBS"',
      copy_rows => FALSE,
      use_existing_object => TRUE);
END;
/
```

Now comes the hard part, how to get the data to the remote site. The difficulty is that the base tables must remain in read-only state until transfer is completed. Any changes and the data at the two sites will be out of synch.

Export, Import Method

The tried and true method is to export the data at the base site, move it across the network, and import it at the remote site. This method was about the only thing available before Oracle9i. By piping the export to a compression program, the dump file can be reduced to speed the movement across the network. The most time consuming part is, of course, the import. Oracle9i introduced a new method called Transportable Tablespaces.

Transportable Tablespaces

Transportable tablespaces allow the DBA to export only the tablespace metadata from the data dictionary and then move the data in datafiles to the remote site. Once the metadata is loaded into the remote site's data dictionary, the tablespace can be used. Since there is no importing of data with the exception of a small amount of metadata, transportable tablespaces can greatly speed-up the process of propagating the initial data to remote master sites. Oracle 10g greatly enhances the transportable tablespace feature to include the ability to move data across different endians and operating systems.

Loading or Re-synchronizing Data

So far, the emphasis has been on moving large amounts of data before creating the replication environment. What if replication has already been created and is running? Replication activity can be stopped on the master group, but that places all objects in the group in read-only status. To stop replication and not place the objects in read-only status, use the *dbms_reputil* package.

```
execute DBMS_REPUTIL.REPLICATION_OFF;
```

This disables all replication triggers so that the data can be modified without replicating the changes. Now data can be loaded or removed without propagating the changes. When finished, reactivate the triggers.

```
execute DBMS_REPUTIL.REPLICATION_ON;
```

Once the replication triggers are active, further changes will be propagated. As always, there is a catch. It is up to the DBA to insure that no user changes are made to any site while the replication triggers are off. Also, to insure data integrity, all sites should load the data simultaneously to avoid conflicts. Data conflicts are covered in the next chapter.

Monitoring Replication with OEM

OEM has become a powerful tool, and where it really shines is in monitoring replication. While signed on as REPADMIN, navigate down to the Advanced Replication Administration folder. OEM displays a graphic of the replication scheme, identifying sites with errors and sites currently propagating transactions (Figure 6.13). The Legend button displays a listing of the different icons.

Figure 6.13 shows that the database link is active and that no master site currently has transactions in the error queue. It also shows that the MYDB.WORLD master site supports 2 tables are replicating to another site as materialized views.

This one quick view provides a detailed report of the replication status. The only detail lacking is the state of the replication jobs at each site. If a job is broken, transactions will build up in the deferred transaction queue, but they will not generate errors. For that reason, scripts like the ones detailed in Chapter 5 should be implemented to monitor jobs at each master site.

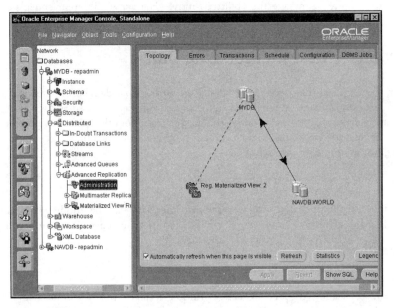

Figure 6.13: *OEM Replication Administration*

Conclusion

This chapter has covered the basics of setting up and administrating a simple multi-master replication scheme, as well as some additional items that need to be considered when planning a multi-master scheme, such as the trusted and untrusted security models. Some of the main points included:

- Plan the implementation in detail. Anticipate how to move the possibly large amounts of data to remote master sites.

- Build the replication and then test it thoroughly.

- DOCUMENT EVERYTHING!!!

- Develop a system to constantly monitor the replication status.

The basics of multi-master replication have been covered. Master sites should be happily replicating transactions back and forth. But the process is still not quite finished. No matter how simple the replication scheme may be, if it involves advanced replication, methods should be implemented to resolve key conflicts. This is what will be covered in the next chapter.

Conflict Avoidance and Resolution

Congratulations! By now, tables should be happily replicating data back and forth. But that is not quite all. If advanced replication is being utilized, steps need to be taken to avoid data conflicts and implement conflict resolution.

No matter how well the replication environment is planned, there are many ways that conflicts with table keys can show up. Any time data is loaded or changed outside the replication environment, such as offline instantiation or data loading, the risk of creating key conflicts exists.

Before placing a replication environment into production, it is imperative to implement conflict resolution to protect data integrity. This chapter will review what conflicts are, how to avoid them, and how to implement an automated way to resolve them. Finally, methods to determine when data is out of synchronization between two tables as well as the methods to resynchronize them will be presented.

What are Conflicts?

The function of a primary key on a single table is easy to understand. The primary key can be used to uniquely identify every row in the table. If you try to insert a row into a table with a primary key and that key already exists in the table, Oracle will reject the new row. In the PUBS database, authors are listed in the *author* table that contains an author key called *auth_key*. This key uniquely identifies each author. This is how to differentiate authors with the same name, like Robert Smith.

Oracle's replication uses this primary key to identify unique rows at all sites containing that table. What about tables without primary keys? All tables in the replication environment contain a key that replication uses to uniquely identify rows across the separate master sites.

Remember, when the master group was created at the master definition site, all tables that did not have a primary key had to have a column or columns identified that uniquely identified rows. Using the SET COLUMNS procedure, a key can be created for Oracle to use in replication. Conflicts happen when data is propagated that violates the key.

To greatly increase the efficiency of replication, Oracle propagates transactions on a schedule. All sites that allow updates, such as updatable Mviews and master sites, will insure that the keys used for replication are not violated. When a row is inserted into a table, the local key is checked, and if the data violates the key, the insert is refused. If the data does not violate the key, it is inserted into the table and the change passes to the deferred transaction queue.

During a push, the data is propagated to other master site deferred transaction queues where the receiver applies them. If the receiver detects that the data violates the key on the local site, it will refuse the transaction and place it in the deferred error queue. This is an example of a conflict. The data is applied at one master site but cannot be applied at another site. At this point, the replicated tables no longer contain the same data.

Key conflicts are just one possible type of replication conflict. When a receiver applies a transaction from the deferred transaction queue, it checks the "before" image to insure that the table data is still the same. What happens when one row of data is updated at two remote sites at the same time? The first update propagates normally and is applied, the second update follows and, because it expects the before image to be the original data, it fails to be applied. The before image is changed by the first update. This is called an update conflict.

A delete conflict is similar; one site updates a row while another site deletes the row. If the update propagates first, the delete fails because the before image does not match. If the delete propagates first, the row no longer exists when the update is applied. As these examples show, getting the replication environment to function is just the beginning. To keep it operating, a plan needs to be in place for conflict avoidance and a method designed to deal with conflict resolution.

Conflict Avoidance

Conflict avoidance is the first step to insure transactions don't end up in the deferred error queues. In planning the replication environment, insure that each master site has the ability to generate unique keys. In the last chapter, two common methods to generate unique keys were covered: assigning blocks of numbers via sequences and attaching a site prefix to a sequence number.

Assigning Blocks of Numbers via Sequences

If a sequence is used to establish a primary key, each site can be assigned a block of numbers to be used for generating a primary key. This is accomplished by setting the sequence at each site to start at a different number.

```
connect pubs/pubs@navdb.world
```

```
create sequence pubs.seq_pk_author
increment by 1
start with 1
maxvalue 99999999
minvalue 1 nocycle
cache 10;


connect pubs/pubs@mydb.world
create sequence pubs.seq_pk_author
increment by 1
start with 100000000
maxvalue 199999999
minvalue 1 nocycle
cache 10;

connect pubs/pubs@newsite.world
create sequence pubs.seq_pk_author
increment by 1
start with 200000000
maxvalue 1.0E28
minvalue 1 nocycle
cache 10;
```

The code above establishes a sequence at three master sites that start at 100,000,000 intervals. With a max value for a sequence equal to 1.0E28, there is a very large pool to divide between the master sites.

There are two key points to remember. First, set up an automated check of the sequences to generate a warning if any site begins to approach *maxvalue*. Second, don't forget the future possibility of adding additional master sites. If the available number is divided equally between all master sites, adding one master site cuts the available number for one site in half to make room for the new site. This issue alone makes this method of generating unique keys less scalable.

Assigning a Prefix Based on Site Name

A more flexible (and scalable) approach is to have all sites start their sequence at 1 and add a site prefix to the sequence number to generate the key.

At NAVDB.WORLD, the first three rows created would have the keys navdb1, navdb2, and navdb3. At the master site MYDB.WORLD, the first three would be *mydb1*, *mydb2*, and *mydb3*. With the site prefix, none of the leys will collide as the rows are propagated.

In real life, keys are not always created on sequences. In cases such as the *author_key* column in the PUBS schema, keys may need to be generated from a central location. All master sites obtain their keys for that table from the central repository. This situation either requires that only that site creates the records or that a procedure be created on the remote site that will fetch the next key from the depository. For efficiency, a trigger could be created that pre-fetches a number of keys and places them in a table and provides them as needed on the local site, fetching additional keys as needed.

> 🔔 It is always a much better solution to use the natural key of the table, if one exists, rather than a derived key. A natural key can avoid a great deal of trouble.

Conflict avoidance must be part of replication planning. Once the replication environment has been created and is operating, it is much harder to avoid conflicts. Also, insure that the conflict avoidance method is flexible enough to handle adding and removing master sites.

However, no matter how diligent one is at planning conflict avoidance, there will eventually be a conflict, and unless conflict resolution is implemented, the replication environment will grind to a halt until there is manual intervention.

Conflict Resolution

Establishing conflict resolution is a process of defining rules for Oracle to apply when a conflict is detected. If the conflict is resolved, the transaction does not end up in the deferred error column group to which the resolution method applies.

There can be multiple column groups on a table and a priority defined for each group. A column group can consist of all the columns in the table or any subset of those columns. Once a column group has been created, one or more conflict resolution methods can be assigned to it. Oracle has defined a number of standard conflict resolution methods that will usually meet be sufficient. The following table provides a list of the different conflict resolution methods Oracle makes available:

METHOD NAME	DESCRIPTION
Latest Timestamp Value	With the latest timestamp value method, define a column that contains a date data type to use in comparing multiple transactions. When a transaction fails because the before image has changed, the column timestamps of the transactions are compared, and if the second transaction is later than the one changing the before image, the second transaction is applied and overlays the current data (which contains the first transaction).
Earliest Timestamp Value	This is the opposite of the above method. The method is available but rarely used.

METHOD NAME	DESCRIPTION
Minimum Value, Maximum Value	When a column group has a conflict between two transactions, the minimum value method evaluates the current and new values of a defined column and selects the lower (or higher for maximum) values to determine if the new columns are applied.
Group Priority Value	In this case, column groups are assigned a priority and conflicts are adjudicated to the highest priority group.
Site Priority Value	In this instance, sites are assigned a priority. When two transactions conflict, the transaction from the master site with the highest priority will be applied. This is actually a special case of the Group Priority Value method above.

 Rollbacks! Conflict Resolution never performs a rollback of a transaction. Since all master sites will contain the same resolution methods, each site should apply the same transactions. If transaction A overwrites transaction B, the site that originally creates transaction B will eventually overwrite it with transaction A. Since all transactions are committed at the originating site, rolling back the transaction is not possible.

What if Oracle is not able to determine which transaction should be applied after using a conflict resolution method? More than one conflict resolution method can be defined. If Oracle is still unable to resolve a conflict after using all defined conflict resolution methods, the transaction ends up in the deferred error queue and someone must manually resolve the conflict.

Examples of Defining Conflict Resolutions

The following section covered creating some of the more common resolution methods in the PUBS schema. First, an example of the latest timestamp conflict resolution method will be examined. Then the site priority conflict resolution method will be looked at.

Defining Latest Timestamp

Conflict resolution methods are defined using the *dbms_repcat.add_update_resolution* procedure. In the following example, Oracle will be configured to use the latest timestamp method of resolution to settle conflicts with the *pubs.sales* table's ORDER_DATE column. This example will:

- Define a column group for use by the resolution method.

- Define the resolution method.

- Add additional support as required.

Here are the steps in more detail.

Define the Column Group

The first step is to define a column group on the master definition site that uses this resolution method.

```
execute dbms_repcat.make_column_group(
    'PUBS','SALES','SALES_COLGP','*');
```

In this example, a column group is defined called SALES_COLGP on the *sales* table in the PUBS schema. This column group will include every column in the table, since the '*' is being used.

It is not necessary to include all columns in the column group. Since the ORDER_DATE column can act as a primary key, it is possible to only define ORDER_DATE in the column group, which would have caused Oracle to resolve only conflicts on that column. By defining all columns in the column group, any conflict within the column group will use the conflict resolution method.

Define the Conflict Resolution Method

Next, define the conflict resolution method for that column group.

```
execute dbms_repcat.add_update_resolution(
    sname  => 'PUBS',
    oname => 'SALES',
    column_group => 'SALES_COLGP',
    sequence => 1,
    method => 'LATEST TIMESTAMP',
    parameter_column_name => 'ORDER_DATE');
```

Now, when a conflict occurs on the column group, the first, and only for the moment, method of resolution will be the latest date method, defined via the *method* parameter. The date within the ORDER_DATE column will be used to resolve the conflict.

To define a second method, the same command can be used, but replace the *method* parameters and change the *sequence* to equal two. Oracle will apply the two conflict resolution methods in the sequence order.

However, the above example has limited usefulness, since the order date is likely to remain the same for all transactions. It would be more useful to compare the transaction execution time, rather than the ORDER_DATE.

> Remember to check *dbms_reputil.from_remote=FALSE* inside the trigger to insure that the trigger does not fire on a transaction from a remote site.

So the replicated object will be altered using the procedure *dbms_repace.alter_master_repobject*, which is called from the master definition site. With this procedure, an additional column will be added to the *sales* table that will be called SALES_TS of type DATE.

```
BEGIN
DBMS_REPCAT.SUSPEND_MASTER_ACTIVITY('REP_GROUP2');
    DBMS_REPCAT.ALTER_MASTER_REPOBJECT(
        sname => '"PUBS"',
        oname => '"SALES"',
        type => 'TABLE',
        ddl_text => -
'alter table PUBS.SALES add (SALES_TS DATE)');
DBMS_REPCAT.RESUME_MASTER_ACTIVITY('REP_GROUP2');
END;
/
```

Now that a new column has been added, it needs to be populated each time some action takes place on the table. Use the following database trigger to perform this action:

```
create trigger SALES_TS_TG
before insert or update
on PUBS.SALES
for each row
begin
  if dbms_reputil.from_remote = FALSE
    then :NEW.SALES_TS := SYSDATE;
  end if;
end;
/
```

Now, replicate the trigger to the other master sites using the *create_master_repobject* procedure. This will ensure the trigger is replicated to all of the master replication sites:

```
BEGIN
DBMS_REPCAT.CREATE_MASTER_REPOBJECT (
  gname => 'REP_GROUP2',
  type => 'TRIGGER',
  oname => 'SALES',
  sname => 'PUBS',
  ddl_text => ' create trigger SALES_TS_TG
      before insert or update
      on PUBS.SALES
      for each row
```

```
      begin
        if dbms_reputil.from_remote = FALSE
          then :NEW.SALES_TS := SYSDATE;
          end if;
   end;');
END;
/
```

Then, redefine the column group and add the conflict resolution method as shown here:

```
execute dbms_repcat.add_update_resolution(
   sname   => 'PUBS',
   oname => 'SALES',
   column_group => 'SALES_COLGP',
   sequence => 1,
   method => 'LATEST TIMESTAMP',
   parameter_column_name => 'SALES_TS');
```

Now replication will function more like a stand-alone database. If two users modify the same data, the data will be applied in the order of commits. In the replication shown here, the two transactions will be applied in the order of the timestamp. This is the most common conflict resolution method.

There is one caveat to consider with this method. All replication database servers must be operating on one time standard. If there are two servers in the replication scheme, one in Virginia and the other in California, the Virginia server time will be four hours ahead of the California server.

Normally databases used in a replication environment use a standard time, either GMT or local time at the company headquarters. It doesn't matter as long as they are the same. A trigger can be created to compensate for the time differences, but the trigger will not be able to be replicated. Instead, the trigger will need to be created at each site, adjusting for the time. The following example shows converting Colorado Mountain Time to GMT.

```
:NEW.LAST_UPDATE := NEW_TIME(SYSDATE,'MDT','GMT');
```

If Oracle was unable to resolve the conflict using the latest timestamp, we could provide an additional resolution method to use. It's called the Site Priority method.

Defining Site Priority

The site priority conflict resolution method uses a column value to determine replication conflict priority. Before starting, replication activities need to be stopped for the group. This is known as a quiesce of the replication group.

Another column is defined in the *pubs.sales* table that will contain an identifier for the site that created the transaction. Next, a trigger is added to insert a site identifier which is usually the database global name. The site priorities need to be defined, using the stored procedure *dbms_repcat.define_site_priority*. Finally, create the column group and define the conflict resolution method.

First, replication needs to be stopped:

```
BEGIN
DBMS_REPCAT.SUSPEND_MASTER_ACTIVITY('REP_GROUP2');
END;
/
```

For this example, the SALES.SALES_SP column (varchar2(30)) is added to use for the site data. An example of adding a column to a replicated table was shown earlier in this chapter. Next, it's time to add the trigger.

```
create trigger SALES_SP_TG
before insert or update
on PUBS.SALES
for each row
declare
  site_name varchar2(30) := -
         dbms_reputil.global_name;
begin
  if dbms_reputil.from_remote = FALSE
    then :NEW.SALES_SP := site_name;
  end if;
end;
/
```

Remember to add the trigger to the replication group so that it is replicated to all master sites. An example of adding triggers to the replication group was provided earlier.

Now, every update or insert transaction will contain the site's global name in the SALES_SP column. A priority needs to be defined for each site in the replication scheme. The *define_site_priority* is the procedure to use:

```
execute dbms_repcat.define_site_priority(
  'REP_GROUP2','SITE_PRI');

execute dbms_repcat.add_site_priority_site('
  REP_GROUP2','SITE_PRI','MYDB.WORLD',10);

execute dbms_repcat.add_site_priority_site('
  REP_GROUP2','SITE_PRI','NAVDB.WORLD',100);

execute dbms_repcat.add_site_priority_site('
  REP_GROUP2','SITE_PRI','NEWSITE.WORLD',5);
```

Here, the priority for each site within the replication scheme is defined. In this example, the master definition site NAVDB.WORLD has the highest priority. A higher number equals higher priority. Notice that they did not have to be created in order, nor does the priority number need to be incremented by one. This comes in handy if it is necessary to add a master site later down the line. At this point, priorities are being assigned to a field in a column, not actual master sites. Thus, it is possible to predefine a priority for a master site that is not yet created.

Now that the master sites priorities have been defined, it is time to define the conflict resolution method.

```
execute dbms_repcat.add_update_resolution(
   sname  => 'PUBS',
   oname => 'SALES',
   column_group => 'SALES_COLGP',
   sequence => 2,
   method => 'SITE PRIORITY',
   parameter_column_name => 'SALES_SP',
   priority_group => 'SITE_PRI');
```

Before resuming replication, it is necessary to regenerate replication support for the *sales* table.

```
execute dbms_repcat.generate_replication_support(
   'PUBS','SALES','TABLE');
```

And finally, resume replication activity to propagate the changes to all other master sites.

```
execute dbms_repcat.resume_master_activity(
   'REP_GROUP2');
```

There are now two methods of conflict resolution defined on the *pubs.sales* table. Oracle will first try to resolve any conflict using the latest timestamp method. If that fails, it will try using the site priority method. If the site priority method fails, the transaction will be placed in the deferred error queue.

Monitoring Conflict Resolution

To monitor conflict resolution, Oracle provides a number of views. First, the object that Oracle is going to maintain statistics on need to be registered.

```
execute dbms_repcat.register_statistics(
   'PUBS','SALES');
```

Information on resolved conflicts can now be obtained from the view *dba_represolution_statistics*.

```
SELECT * FROM dba_represolution_statistics;
```

dba_represolution_statistics contains the following fields.

```
Name                     Null?     Type
------------------------- --------- -----------
SNAME                    NOT NULL  VARCHAR2(30)
ONAME                    NOT NULL  VARCHAR2(30)
CONFLICT_TYPE                      VARCHAR2(10)
REFERENCE_NAME           NOT NULL  VARCHAR2(30)
METHOD_NAME              NOT NULL  VARCHAR2(80)
FUNCTION_NAME                      VARCHAR2(92)
PRIORITY_GROUP                    VARCHAR2(30)
RESOLVED_DATE            NOT NULL  DATE
PRIMARY_KEY_VALUE        NOT NULL  VARCHAR2(2000)
```

As conflicts are resolved, rows are added to the view. To remove the statistics, they need to be purged.

```
execute dbms_repcat.purge_statistics(
  'PUBS','SALES');
```

To stop gathering resolution statics on the *sales* table:

```
execute dbms_repcat.cancel_statistics(
  'PUBS','SALES');
```

Of course, data on conflicts that are not resolved is in the deferred error queue and can be found in the *deferror* view.

```
select * from deferror;
```

Using OEM to define Conflict Resolution methods

Oracle Enterprise Manager can not only create column groups and define conflict resolution, but it presents the information in a fairly comprehensive way. While OEM is wholeheartedly recommended for monitoring multi-master replication, it is not recommended for creating multi-master replication and conflict resolution.

Because of the complex nature and multiple layers of conflict resolution, it is recommended scripts be created that document methods, column groups, etc. OEM will create conflict resolution without allowing documentation of what and how it was created.

Keeping this in mind, the following looks at how OEM creates the latest timestamp conflict resolution method on the *pubs.sales* table.

Log on to OEM as REPADMIN and navigate to the replication group created in the last chapter, REP_GROUP2. Submit a stop request to quiesce replication activity. Expand the REP_GOUP2 folder and select the *pubs.store* table.

First, add a column to the *store* table called STORE_TS. Select the Alter Object tab and enter the DDL to add the column and select apply. Now, create the trigger and add it to the replication master group.

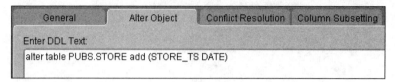

Figure 7.2: *OEM Adding a Column to the store table*

Select "*Column Subsetting*" to define the column group. The only column group defined is the Shadow Group, which is an internal group that contains all columns in the table. Once a column group is defined, the shadow group will disappear. Select the Create button to open the Create Column Group window. Name the column group STORE_CG. Select all the columns and move them to the right hand pane with the right arrow button.

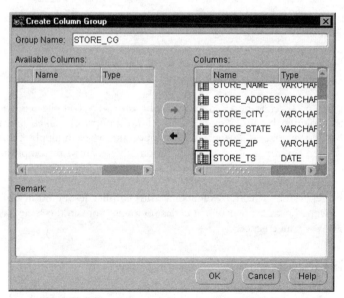

Figure 7.3: *OEM Create Column Group*

Select OK to create the STORE_CG column group. Once the group is created, highlight it and select the Add button in the Column Group Resolution Methods text box to bring up the Edit Resolutions Methods Window. Select the Latest Timestamp and STORE_TS from the combo boxes and select OK to create the method.

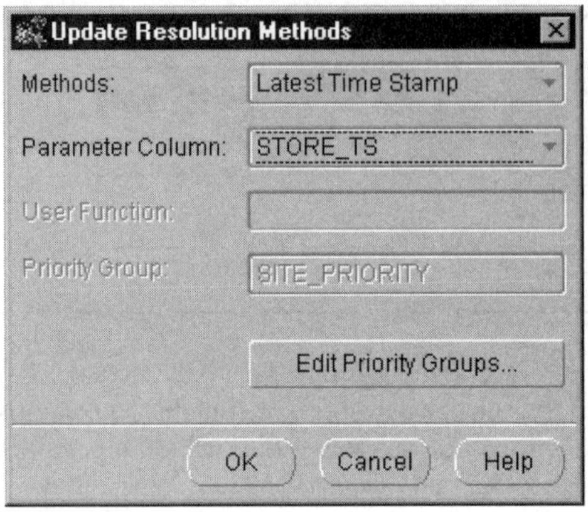

Figure 7.4: *OEM Update Resolution Methods*

The final task is to again generate replication support for the *store* table and then resume replication activity.

Setting up conflict resolution using OEM is relatively painless; however, there is no documentation trail, such as a script, to allow the recreation of the scheme if needed.

As shown here, advanced replication can and does become very complicated, with multiple conflict resolution methods defined on column groups, on tables, and in master groups. Documentation becomes very important when multiple DBAs support the replication environment. As the replication scheme grows in complexity, scripts to recreate and document it become an important asset.

At this point, the replication scheme is functional with conflict resolution in place. The last area to cover is what happens when tables no longer contain the same data. This is called Data Mis-convergence.

Data Mis-convergence

Data Mis-convergence happens when the data in the tables does not match. This should never happen, but it will, so there needs to be a plan to resynchronize the data. If the same number of rows exist in the replicated tables, then the data mis-convergence was caused by updates performed while replication was turned off using *dbms_reputil.replication_off.*

There are a number of ways to resynchronize the data in the tables. When the data is out of sync, any update will generate a conflict, because the before image is not what is expected. A last timestamp conflict resolution method will automatically resolve the conflict and re-sync the data with the latest update.

If knowledgeable about the replication scheme, a DBA may update all the timestamp fields on a table to force all the rows to propagate the data from the correct table, re-synchronizing the remote tables.

Using the *dbms_rectifier_diff* package

One way to determine if the data is out of synch is to use the *dbms_rectifier_diff* package that comes with Oracle9i. This package compares the data at a master site, although not necessarily the master definition site, with the data at a remote master site. It loads any discrepancies it finds into a user created table and can then use that data to synchronize the two tables.

In this example the *author* table at NAVDB.WORLD will be compared to the *author* table at MYDB.WORLD. The first step is to create a couple of tables to hold the data found by the *differences* procedure.

```
connect repadmin/repadmin@navdb.world

create table PUBS.MISSING_ROWS_AUTHOR (
   AUTHOR_KEY           VARCHAR2(11),
   AUTHOR_LAST_NAME     VARCHAR2(40),
   AUTHOR_FIRST_NAME    VARCHAR2(20),
   AUTHOR_PHONE         VARCHAR2(12),
   AUTHOR_STREET        VARCHAR2(40),
   AUTHOR_CITY          VARCHAR2(20),
   AUTHOR_STATE         VARCHAR2(2),
   AUTHOR_ZIP           VARCHAR2(5),
   AUTHOR_CONTRACT_NBR NUMBER(5));

 create table PUBS.MISSING_LOCATION_AUTHOR (
   present    VARCHAR2(128),
   absent     VARCHAR2(128),
   r_id              ROWID);
```

The first table matches the definition of the *author* table so that it can hold a complete row of data. The second table must be defined as shown. Next, replication activity should be suspended.

```
dbms_repcat.suspend_master_activity(
   'REP_GROUP2');
```

Now execute the stored procedure *dbms_rectifier_diff.differences* to determine if rows are not in sync between the two tables.

```
execute dbms_rectifier_diff.differenced(
  sname1                    => 'PUBS',
  oname1                    => 'AUTHOR',
  reference_site            => 'NAVDB.WORLD',
  sname2                    => 'PUBS',
  oname2                    => 'AUTHOR',
  comparison_site           => 'MYDB.WORLD',
  where_clause              => NULL,
  column_list               => NULL,
  missing_rows_sname        => 'PUBS',
  missing_rows_oname1       => 'MISSING_ROWS_AUTHOR',
  missing_rows_oname2       => 'MISSING_LOCATION_AUTHOR',
  missing_rows_site => 'NAVDB.WORLD',
  max_missing               => 500,
  comit_rows                => 100);
```

Using a NULL in the *column_list* parameter will cause all columns to be used. The rows that are out of sync between the two tables are contained in the *missing_rows_author* table. This information can be used to manually fix the data or Oracle can re-sync the two tables.

To have Oracle resynchronize the two tables, run the *dbms_rectifier_diff.rectify* procedure. Oracle will resynchronize the remote table with the local table. The local table's data will not be changed. Oracle will insert the missing rows and delete the rows that are not contained in the local table.

Caution should be taken when using *rectify*'s resynchronization methodology. It is important that these procedures be run from the location that has the correct data. *differences* must be run before *rectify*.

```
dbms_rectifier_diff.rectify(
  sname1            => 'PUBS',
  oname1            => 'AUTHOR',
  reference_site    => 'NAVDB.WORLD',
  sname2            => 'PUBS',
  oname2            => 'AUTHOR',
  comparison_site   => 'MYDB.WORLD',
  column_list              => NULL,
  missing_rows_sname  => 'PUBS',
  missing_rows_oname1 => 'MISSING_ROWS_AUTHOR',
  missing_rows_oname2 => 'MISSING_LOCATION_AUTHOR' ,
  missing_rows_site => 'NAVDB.WORLD',
  comit_rows               => 100);
```

The last point about the *dbms_rectifier_diff* package is that both procedures may take an extremely long time to execute. It may be a better option to just re-instantiate the remote table using transportable tablespaces or an export of the local table.

Conclusion

This chapter contains a lot of complex procedures to insure the integrity of data in the replication environment. The key topics were Conflict Avoidance, Conflict Resolution, and Data Mis-convergence.

- **Conflict Avoidance** – Plan the replication environment from the start to insure conflicts are rare. Do not rely on only one site updating and inserting data. Insure the replication plan is flexible enough to allow for adding or remove master sites.

- **Conflict Resolution** – A few of the most common methods of automatic conflict resolution were introduced and the steps that are required implementing them. Remember that conflict resolution allows Oracle to determine which transactions are applied when conflicts arise. If Oracle is unable to make that determination, the transaction is placed in the local deferred error queue and replication begins to fail.

- **Data Mis-convergence** – Re-synchronizing tables in a replication environment can be a daunting task. Oracle9i provides the *dbms_rectifier_diff* package to help determine if the tables are no longer synchronized. However, for large data sets, it may be advantageous to reconstruct the replication table due to the time it will take the *rectify* procedure to run.

That's it. Both basic and advanced replication have been implemented, as well as monitoring scripts and conflict resolution. This information set the foundation for planning and creating a replication environment.

This has not been an exhaustive examination of Oracle replication, nor was it meant to be. The goal was to provide the basics, identify some of the pitfalls, and give working examples that facilitate implementing replication.

Remember to start in a test environment. Plan out the types of replication needed and don't implement multi-master replication unless it is dictated by requirements. Also, document each step. Remember, someone else may have to support or rebuild the replication scheme.

Introduction to Oracle Data Guard

Introduction to Oracle Data Guard

Oracle has been advertised as a bulletproof system, but achieving bulletproof status will require several components.

These components make up Oracle's High Availability (HA) infrastructure, a set of tools that provide protection from different types of interruption or downtime.

This section is an overview that will summarize different types of downtime and Oracle tools that allow the DBA to protect against them. Oracle Dataguard will be covered specifically as a method to prevent excessive downtime, data loss, or more damaging types of outages such as server room loss.

Types of Failures

Downtime comes in two main forms, each presenting different issues for the DBA and the business.

Unplanned Downtime

This type of downtime occurs without warning and can range from mildly disruptive to disastrous. Examples of unplanned downtime include:

- Instance Failure

- Server (Host) Failure

- Data Failure

- Data Center Loss

Instance failures can occur when an Oracle instance crashes due to an internal error, such as an ORA-600, that results in a failure of Oracle's processes. A user with operating system privileges may also cause an instance failure by inadvertently killing one of Oracle's five required background processes. Though disruptive, an instance failure is a mild issue, as it can be resolved simply by starting the database.

Oracle Replication

Server, or host failure, is roughly the same, except that it involves the entire system crashing. This can occur when an operating system experiences a critical error, such as a kernel panic, resulting in the entire server aborting. Like the instance failure, this can be resolved by the DBA using a simple *startup* command. However, this issue can result in more downtime since a system's administrator is usually required to bring the operating system back online and processes such as *fsck* must run to ensure proper system integrity.

Data failure is the worst of the three, resulting in the loss or corruption of data. Some disk failures are non-disastrous; for instance, if a disk is mirrored with hardware or software RAID. Even then, if excessive disks are lost it is possible that production data could be lost as well, requiring some form of recovery. User error can also cause data loss if an operating system user removes database files with a command such as *rm*. In this case, the file will be removed, and the disk mirror will provide no protection. Lastly, corruption can occur if hardware or software bugs result in inappropriate data being written to the datafiles.

Data Center Loss occurs when a system is completely lost, usually as the result of some sort of natural disaster. A hurricane, flood, or tornado may destroy or seriously disable an entire data center resulting in a combined loss of servers and disk. This is by far the worst unplanned-downtime scenario, and can only be protected against with extensive (and usually expensive) disaster recovery methods.

Planned Downtime

This downtime is planned by the DBA and should be less disruptive than unplanned downtime in most cases. Examples of planned downtime include:

- Schema-level Changes
- System-level Changes

Schema-level changes resulting in downtime usually involve reorganization of tables or tablespaces. However, downtime can also be caused by smaller changes that interrupt service to key tables such as index reorganizations, dropping columns, or validating constraints.

System-level changes resulting in downtime include patches and upgrades, migrations, and anything else that requires a shutdown of the Oracle database. Other examples may include switching to archivelog mode or moving a critical datafile.

Data Guard was introduced as the Standby Database in Oracle 7.3, and has evolved significantly since then. Ideally, Data Guard provides a combined solution for the problem of high availability and disaster recovery without compromising performance.

This chapter provides an overview of Oracle Data Guard technology. It includes basic information on standby databases. This information will help DBAs decide if Oracle Data Guard is the appropriate solution, in the realm of disaster protection and high availability, for their enterprise.

Oracle High Availability Options

Oracle provides many options for preventing downtime and data loss, all of which make up the Maximum Availability Architecture (MAA). The MAA provides redundancy on all components and employs different Oracle tools.

These tools must protect systems from planned and unplanned downtime. In addition, it must protect systems from varying levels of unplanned downtime ranging from single server outages to entire data center loss.

Some businesses choose not to follow all the guidelines for maximum availability. When considering a high availability strategy, the DBA must consider:

- Recovery Time Objective (RTO)

- Recovery Point Objective (RPO)

- Downtime Cost-per-Minute

- Available Resources

The RTO defines the allowable downtime for the database. An advertising company may allow hours of downtime; however, a bank will usually allow no downtime whatsoever. RPO defines the allowable data loss if a failure occurs. If batch processes load the data, it may be that hours or even days of data could be reloaded. However, for a system that allows direct access by the end user, such as an online store or ATM machine, zero data loss is allowed.

Downtime can be expensive. Depending on the system, costs can range from dollars per minute to tens-of-thousands of dollars lost for every minute the database is unavailable.

Oracle provides two primary methods for achieving high availability through failover: Real Application Clusters (RAC) and Data Guard. Both of these options will incur different downtimes, configuration costs, and expenses.

Real Application Clusters - The RAC architecture allows many instances to share a single database through shared storage. This architecture provides the Cache Fusion product which allows these instances to transfer data buffers between nodes (servers) using a high-speed low-latency network interconnect. RAC works closely with Oracle's Transparent Application Failover (TAF) to automatically restart any connections when an instance fails. This method of high availability protects the database against instance failure, server failure, and some planned outages such as patches. With TAF, users will be able to enjoy continuous 24x7 usage with little to no downtime.

Oracle Data Guard - This is a free option with Oracle Enterprise Edition, providing an automated standby database. In a configuration allowing maximum protection against failure, the standby database is an exact block-for-block copy of the primary database that is kept up to date with redo log information. Upon server failure, a series of database procedures synchronizes the standby database and opens it to accept connections.

Now that information on the two primary options for high availability have been presented, a closer look at the Data Guard method in particular will be covered.

Types of Standby Databases

Standby databases can be categorized as either a physical standby database or a logical standby database depending on the method used to propagate changes from the primary database.

A physical standby database has the identical structure of the primary database on a block-per-block basis, whereas a logical standby database does not need to be an exact replica of the primary database. In addition to these two primary types, the standby database can be configured to act as archive log repository.

Physical Standby Database

The physical standby database is an exact copy of the primary database on a block-per-block basis. The archived redo logs on a physical database are applied using the physical row values. Hence, all the segments in the primary and the standby database will be the same.

The physical database can be in recovery mode or read-only mode, but it cannot operate in both modes at the same time. When in recovery mode, the archived redo logs from the primary database are applied to keep it current and in sync with the primary database. When in read-only mode the standby database can be used for reporting or any other non-DML actions.

The physical standby database in read-only mode can never be open for DML, because DML and committing in a standby database new redo; therefore, further recovery will not be possible.

In a physical data guard environment, the archive redo logs from the primary database are transferred automatically to the standby database using the standard Oracle networking structures (server connection data and listeners). The logs are then applied to the standby database by log apply services; therefore, there is no need for manual intervention. The details of the processes involved in the transfer and application of redo logs to the standby database are given in the book "Oracle Data Guard" by Rampant TechPress.

A standby database in read-only mode is used for ad-hoc reporting and can be very useful for offloading some of the reporting tasks from the primary database. In this mode, the archived redo logs cannot be applied to the standby database, and at this point, the primary and the standby databases diverge. If there is only one standby database in the configuration, the DBA should be very protective about the archived redo logs as long as the standby database is in read-only mode. If a single archive log is lost before being applied to the standby, the standby must be re-instantiated from a fresh copy of the primary database datafiles.

The mode of operation of standby databases can be changed between recovery mode and read-only mode and vice versa; however, the standby database can only be in one mode at a time.

The physical standby database performs better than the logical standby database because it uses media recovery to apply archived redo logs. Moreover, there are fewer limitations on a physical standby database compared to a logical standby database.

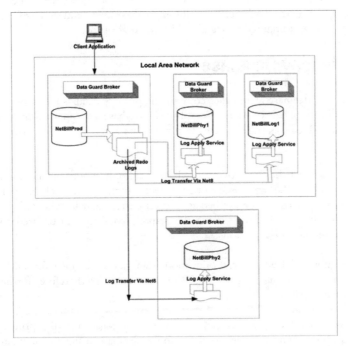

Figure 8.1: *A Sample Data Guard Configuration*

Logical Standby Database

The logical standby database was introduced in Oracle 9i and has been enhanced significantly by Oracle 10g. A logical standby database can contain all or a set of objects from the primary database. In addition, it can be a mixture of a few objects from the primary database and few objects of its own. For instance, a logical standby database can contain materialized views and indexes that are not present on the primary server, allowing much more sophisticated usage such as decision support systems or data warehouses. As a result, data manipulation on the primary database will not incur extra overhead resulting from updating indexes and refreshing materialized views. The overhead will instead occur on the standby server, which is more acceptable to the DBA.

The data in a logical standby database is kept current using the SQL apply mode. In SQL apply mode, the SQL statements from archived redo logs are extracted using LogMiner technology and are then applied to the standby database. The main difference between physical and logical standby databases is that a logical database is always open and is "recovered" when it is open, whereas a physical standby database can be either open or in recovery mode, but never both at the same time.

A logical standby database can be open in read/write mode. Database objects that are not replicated from the primary database, and therefore exclusive to the standby database, can be updated. The objects to be updated by the log apply service can only be in read only mode to ensure the consistency of data between a logical standby and the primary database.

Unlike a physical standby database, a logical standby database does not support all data types. Data types such as BFILE, VARRAY, ROWID, UROWID, XMLTYPE, and user-defined types are not supported in logical standby databases. In addition, encrypted columns and multimedia types such as Oracle Text or Spatial are not supported. During the SQL apply on a logical database, any attempt to update data in a table containing columns of an unsupported data type will return error, and the log apply service will terminate. *dba_logstdby_unsupported* view can be used on the primary database to find out if the database contains any unsupported data types.

Theoretically, a logical standby database can be used as the primary database during an outage on the true primary database. Since a logical standby database may not contain all the objects from the primary database, the switchover to the logical standby database may restrict the services offered by the true primary database. As a result, the DBA should carefully consider the objects to be replicated in a logical standby database during the configuration phase if the logical standby is to be used as a high availability method.

Archive Log Repository

Sometimes, the standby database configuration is used only as an archive log repository. In this case, the benefit is the storage of the archived redo logs on another server for a small period of time. Oracle processes, using standard networking components, maintain the transfer of archived redo logs. For an archive log repository configuration, data files are not required; therefore, it cannot be used for data recovery.

Benefits and Drawbacks of Data Guard

Like any technology, Data Guard has advantages and disadvantages. Data Guard configuration has the advantages of disaster protection, load balancing, and automated management. These will be covered in more detail in the following sections.

Disaster Protection

A physical Data Guard environment provides protection against server loss, data loss, and even server room loss. Data Guard is Oracle's top Disaster Recovery (DR) solution, providing the capability to ship data to other parts of the world that may not be prone to the same disasters as your primary data center.

Data Guard can use several standby databases in different areas of the world. No matter how many databases are employed, the same concepts apply: archive logs are generated on the primary and shipped using the Oracle network. The standby database is responsible for the automatic recovery of the new log. Because the log recovery on the standby will not be real-time, there is usually a lag in the standby database, where it falls behind the primary database depending on how often redo logs switch. However, this lag can work for the DBA. If user error occurs, such as an end-user keying in a large mistake, the Data Guard connection can be broken before the change is allowed to propagate to the standby database.

Moreover, a Data Guard environment can be configured in three different modes: maximum protection, maximum availability, and maximum performance. The DBA must evaluate the requirements of their enterprise to configure Data Guard in one of these modes to suit the chosen disaster recovery strategy.

In addition to disaster protection, standby databases can be used for database services during the planned outage of the primary database for maintenance work. By using Data Guard Manager (*dgmgrl*), the DBA can perform easy switchovers from the primary database to any standby. A switchback can be performed when the old primary is once again prepared to handle operations. This ability assists with planned downtime; particularly outages involving upgrades to hardware or the OS of the primary database.

Load Balancing

Standby databases can contribute towards load balancing on the primary database. The ad-hoc reporting and backup operation activities can be off loaded to the standby database, reducing load on the primary database.

The physical standby database can be opened in read-only mode and will cater to the DBA's reporting requirements. Careful consideration is required when selecting the operating mode because as long as a physical standby database is open in read-only mode, it cannot be synchronized with the primary database.

As a result, the most up-to-date data will not be available for reporting. If the reporting requirements of the organization demand the most up-to-date information from the primary database or real-time data, a logical standby database will be a more proper choice. A logical standby database is always open in read-only or read/write mode and can keep the data in sync with the primary database while providing reporting services.

If the backup and recovery strategy includes a traditional online or offline backup of the database along with Data Guard configuration, the backup operation can be offloaded from the primary database to the standby database. Because the standby database is a block-for-block copy of the primary database, a backup taken from the standby is still recoverable to the point of failure using archive logs generated on the primary server.

Automated Management

Managed recovery mode for standby databases greatly reduces the amount of time a DBA has to spend on setting up a failover environment. In managed recovery mode, the archived redo logs are automatically transferred from the primary database to the standby database and applied to the standby database.

The only time a DBA needs to monitor and maintain the standby database is if there are gaps in the archived redo logs on the standby site. However, this is usually taken care of by a service called FAL (Fetch Archive Log). This service will perform gap detection and resolve them as necessary.

Even when DBA intervention is necessary, it is made easier by Data Guard Broker. The Data Guard Broker framework provides a GUI and command line interface to monitor, administer, and deploy Data Guard configurations.

Data Guard Downsides

The following issues are applicable in a Data Guard configuration:

- Servers running the primary and standby databases should have the same version of Oracle software.

- Servers running the primary and standby databases should have the same release of operating system software.

- The primary database should run in FORCE LOGGING mode to avoid any divergence of data between the primary and the standby database as a result of unrecoverable writes on the primary database.

- The Data Guard option is only available in the Enterprise Edition of Oracle Database software.

Lifecycle of a Standby Database

Lifecycle of a standby database in a Data Guard environment can be depicted using Figure 8.2.

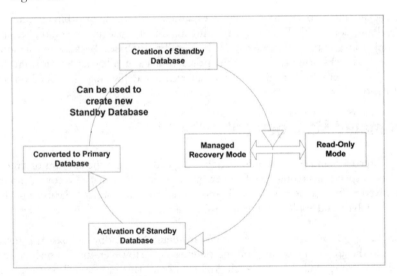

Figure 8.2: *Lifecycle of a Standby Database*

The following sections cover the stages in the life of a standby database.

Creation of Standby Database

A standby database is created from a backup of the primary database. Backup database files, as hot backups or an RMAN backup, and standby control files are transferred to the standby database site, thus forming the standby database. A client-server connection is established between the primary and the standby database to facilitate the transfer of archived redo logs.

Also, the initialization parameters on the primary and standby databases respective SPFILES are configured for node identification to be used by log transfer services. Once these changes are made, the standby database can be started in recovery mode.

Recovery or read-only mode

After the creation of the standby database, the log transfer service can be started on the primary database to transfer the archived logs to the standby database. The log apply service on the standby database applies the archived redo logs to keep the database in sync with the primary database. These two services form an important part in the life cycle of the standby database.

In the case of a physical standby environment, the standby database can be opened for read-only (query) processing. During any time period where the physical standby database is open in read-only mode, the log apply service remains idle and does not apply the archived redo logs to the standby database; however, the log transfer service continues to transfer archived logs from the primary to the standby database. These logs are applied to the physical standby database when it is placed in recovery mode again. If any archive logs are lost due to space constraints, the standby database will have to be re-instantiated by repeating the creation phase.

Switchover or failover operation

The standby database will be activated to serve as the primary database at some point in its life cycle. There are normally two situations when this operation will be performed: a planned outage for maintenance of the primary database or an unplanned outage such as a disaster situation. A switchover operation occurs when a standby database is transitioned into the primary database role and the primary database into the standby database role. In the switchover operation, no data is lost and the Data Guard configuration remains.

The switchover operation is performed for maintenance of the primary database. However, in the case of an unplanned outage on the primary site, the standby database will be activated as a primary database without gracefully switching roles on the primary server. This is called failover. There are two types of failover operations:

Graceful or "no-data-loss" failover and Forced or "minimal-data-loss" failover. Once the standby database is transitioned into primary database status in either switchover or failover, the life of the database as the standby ends and its service as the primary database begins.

Standby Database in Standard Edition

Oracle Standby Databases require archive logs to be shipped to the standby server. The standby database takes these archive logs and processes them, thereby bringing the system up to date since the last redo log switch.

As such, an automated Dataguard system cannot be set up using Oracle Standard Edition (SE). Oracle SE only allows for a single archive log destination, which must be local. Enterprise Edition, on the other hand, allows for ten destinations, which is more than enough to create local and remote copies.

To provide a standby method for Oracle SE, the DBA must create OS level log shipping scripts. These scripts must detect when the Oracle ARCn process is finished writing an archive log. The script must then take the resulting archive log and copy it to the standby server using a method such as FTP, RCP, or SCP (secure). This standby server remains in RECOVER DATABASE mode, and will therefore accept the new archive log and recovery itself up to date.

While this method can save money by using Oracle SE, there are a few downsides:

- A license must still be purchased for the standby database

- If a node fails, data that has not been written to archive logs may be lost

- Recovery can take time depending on when the primary database crashed

- Client connection configurations, such as *tnsnames.ora*, must be manually changed to recognize the new database as the primary.

Oracle Streams Replication

9

This is an excerpt from the book *Oracle Streams* by Rampant TechPress, which can be purchased from www.rampant.cc.

Introduction to Streams Replication

In this introductory chapter, an overview of some key concepts of data sharing and data synchronization needs that originate both within and outside of enterprises will be presented. How the Oracle Stream technology fits into the data sharing realm will also be examined.

Oracle Streams provides a queue-based and non-intrusive methodology that can be used to transfer the changed data across databases. It offers a new method of data replication for the Oracle Database environment. It is asynchronous in nature and as a result, it has minimum impact on the source database system. In keeping with market demand, Oracle has developed this revolutionary stream replication method which reads the redo logs with the intent of capturing the database transactions for onwards propagation and consumption. This is a timely departure for the Oracle database environment which hitherto depended on trigger snapshot replication and synchronous advanced replication

Streams replication is the new kid on the block!!

There is a strong and growing need for data sharing among the different internal and external users in an organization. This is becoming more important due to the rapid globalization of business operations. Oracle Streams is well positioned to offer a simple and flexible, yet revolutionary, method to move data between databases at high speeds. Streams based replication involves data exchange between the peer database systems. It readily provides an alternate database, which can serve as the primary whenever the original primary database is lost or inoperable. In a way, it can be designed to be disaster recovery solution. For performance reasons, the destination database which is maintained by the Streams replication process can be used as the access point for many of the applications because the data resides in the near vicinity of the application location. The flexibility and overall utility of the Streams processes are what make it a database revolution.

Data Sharing and Replication

Data accumulation usually happens where business operations normally occur. As a result, there are often islands of data within the organization. Even though there is usually some effort within organizations to consolidate and reduce the number of data centers and database systems, the existing systems are often resident in varied platforms and operating systems.

The situation involving multiple databases located in different geographical areas necessitates data sharing. While data explosion and data accumulation is occurring at one end of the system, the need for sharing the same data is growing with equal speed on the data access end of the system. With global operations becoming the order of the day, data sharing and data duplication are becoming significant aspects of data management. This is where data replication plays a key role. With the help of methods such as Oracle Streams, data movement is organized and the sharing of up-to-date data is made possible for more users. Streams replication, for instance, is capable of transferring the database transactions in near real time to the destination site.

The maintenance of a data replica site in a remote location or in a distributed environment allows the system to fail over to the replicated site when the need arises. The replicated data also serves a key role in disaster recovery as Streams can be configured to ensure that the risk of losing data is very small.

Global Streams Operations

When the Internet is combined with advancements in networking technology, computer systems are able to communicate very effectively across countries and continents. Globalization of business activity is a primary benefit of the expanded and innovative IT infrastructure. With the help of improved communication facilities and better IT systems, business organizations are able to transact globally.

To meet the goal of globalization of trade and commerce, database systems need to be fully geared up for providing the information and analytical capability. As operations tend to spread across states and countries with offices located in different geographical areas, data availability in the various office locations becomes an important issue. This accentuates the common and essential need for data sharing. Even though the business or corporate data is collected and stored in different locations, all data has to be made available to IT applications running at these many business locations. Data replication, based on methods such as Oracle Streams, provides the necessary infrastructure for effective data movement and data sharing across distances great and small.

For instance, the corporate head office located in Chicago would be interested in monitoring and tracking product distribution through information on daily sales and inventory levels from its country wide offices. The Streams based data replication method would configure data movement to the corporate database system asynchronously.

The country-wide data could be monitored in a near real-time way, thus helping the sales and inventory analysis in timely manner so that adjustments in other business processes could be made to increase income for the corporation. In another instance, traders located in the London and Singapore offices of a financial services organization would like keep track of the trades and price movement executed in New York location for derivative products.

Data replication conducted using the Streams replication process is an ideal choice for achieving the above mentioned objectives. Users in all locations would have the updated information in a time efficient manner. Worldwide decisions could be made effectively because all users would be confident that they had the best data on which to base their business decisions.

Data Synchronization

As the need for data sharing and data movement to desired locations and application sites is evaluated, one prominent goal of the effort would be data synchronization.

Since it is more and more likely that the data will be pulled from a variety of internal and external locations, there is a need to examine the ways in which each data set is synchronized or refreshed. Assuming that the accumulated data from one location is needed for other locations, the data has to be moved, transformed, and/or replicated. All of these methods of data handling are generally used within any given organization. Each of these methods is applicable in different circumstances.

Oracle Streams is well-equipped to perform such data synchronization. For example, Streams has built-in flexibility that allows the design of apply handlers and on-the-fly data transformation methodologies. When multiple sites participate in the data transfers, the goal should be to have the data from other sites as soon as new data available. Streams can move the data and synchronize it at multiple sites.

Data Replication

Data Replication is the process in which the data is duplicated at the destination database. Data Replication is normally a built-in methodology in all relational database systems. Some relational database products even support replication to heterogeneous database systems.

A typical Data Replication process captures the changes at the source database and applies those changes at the destination database in a continuous or scheduled manner. There are many reasons why data replication is a widely used database option. Some of the main reasons are as follows:

Global Organizations - An organization operating at multiple locations often needs all of the data to be available at every location. Data may be accumulated and maintained at remote sites which are not accessible for the applications. As a result, the local application requires its own data site. In such a situation, the data is sent by using data replication methodology.

Site Autonomy - In many situations, the local sites run their own applications and want to maintain their own data, but they also want to get the remote data on a periodic or continuous basis. The data replication process can help achieve the data independence by obtaining the necessary data from the remote locations.

Enhanced Performance - For performance reasons, the data is often maintained close to the application that is processing it. Remote access to the data may involve additional network traffic delays. Centralizing application access from various locations to a common database may have a huge impact on the performance of the database. By maintaining the independent data locations or database systems, yet synchronized from remote database systems, application performance is generally improved.

Availability and Data Protection - By maintaining the replicated database site, an indirect benefit of data protection is achieved. Since the replication is a peer-to-peer system, the infrastructure facility of the remote database system provides true database system availability. When the remote system is located in a distant place, it can very well act as the disaster recovery database system. When the local database system is unavailable due to an unforeseen catastrophe, the remote database is kept up-to-date by the replication process and can easily provide the database service.

Oracle's Streams based replication was developed to address all of the above mentioned objectives. The Streams process is so comprehensive that it has become Oracle's preferred method and technology for conducting data replication both within and outside the Oracle database environment. Knowing that the worldwide thirst for current data is only going to grow, Oracle is committed to supporting, developing and enhancing its database's features further.

What is Oracle Streams?

Oracle Streams is Oracle database's new method of data sharing. Oracle Streams provides a mechanism for the propagation of database changes within the database or to the external database system. Oracle Streams, simply called Streams, keeps track of all the database changes in terms of Data Manipulation Language (DML) commands and Data Definition Language (DDL) commands. It then stages those changes into queues and later moves them to the destination queues where they are applied to the destination database objects.

Streams provides a flow mechanism in which the database changes flow in a streamed manner, hence the name Streams. Besides the database changes, Streams can also capture user defined events, stage them, and apply them at the destination database. To apply changes means that based on the specification or rules defined, the changes can be made at the destination. In fact, they are consummated at the destination site. As shown in Figure 9.1, Streams provides a data flow mechanism which continuously keeps moving and transferring messages. This becomes the basis for many data sharing and messaging functions.

Streams Information Flow

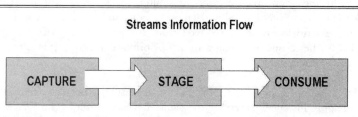

Figure 9.1: *Simplistic View of Streams Data Flows*

Typically, the capture of database changes involves extracting changes made to the tables, schema, or entire database objects by reading the redo log files. Redo Log Files record all changes made to the database object whether they are rolled back or committed.

All the captured changes are converted into events called Logical Change Records (LCR). The Capture process enqueues them into the appropriate queues. Besides scanning and extracting the changes, there is another facility where user applications can explicitly create events. This can be LCR(s) or user messages. These are known as user-enqueued events.

Streams provides a rich set of methods that allow DBAs to control what kind of data and information is placed into Streams and how the stream flows or is routed from one system to another. There are rules, transformations, and configurations that control the entire flow of capture and apply.

Where to use Streams Replication

The Oracle Streams methodology provides an integrated infrastructure in which a variety of messaging functions and data flow systems are implemented. Streams Methodology supports Oracle functions such as message queuing through advanced queuing, data replication, event management and notification, data warehousing loading, and data protection by way of the standby database.

How do the Streams differ from the Oracle Data Guard solution and the Oracle RAC solution? Both the Streams replication process and Data Guard rely on the same underlying technology. Both of these read the redo log files for the database changes. Database transactions are recorded in the redo log files. In the case of Data Guard, the transactions are extracted by the log transport service. In the Streams process, the changes are extracted by the capture process.

The Data Guard solution focuses primarily on providing a standby database. It is more of an Oracle provided Disaster Recovery (DR) solution. The Data Guard database is a peer host system with an independent database that can be put into use immediately in the event the primary, or source, database is lost or rendered inoperable. The Data Guard standby database is constantly kept in recovery mode and the all the redo log changes received from the primary database are applied regularly. It has one-to-one matching with that of primary database. It is fairly simple to configure and maintain.

A Real Application Cluster (RAC) database is basically a parallel database with clustered multiple instances accessing the same database system. The Oracle RAC database system offers scalability and high availability solutions. Scalability is achieved in that multiple instances can be added, each with its own host resources aimed at meeting the ever-increasing user transaction load. High availability is a built-in feature of the RAC database. Since the database can be accessed and handled through any one of the instances, failure of the host does not cause database failure or database service loss. The Oracle RAC database system uses shared storage to host the database structures.

Oracle Streams offers a different solution that is broader in its perspective. Streams based replication can provide an alternative data source. It is a much more flexible solution than the Data Guard solution in that it is designed to do more than simply provide a standby database for failover or disaster recovery; although, it can very well act as the DR solution. Since Streams is a pure data solution, data can be maintained as either a complete replica of the source database or as a subset of the data. With Streams, data can be transformed as desired and can also be sent to multiple destinations. With the help of apply handlers, a variety of data transformations are possible. In addition, auditing routines can be developed and tracked. PL/SQL routines can be devised to drive the data transformations based on the needs of the users.

RAC, Data Guard and Streams offer different solutions. Each methodology has its strengths, but the Streams methodology has cleverly incorporated some of the strengths of RAC and Data Guard.

Message Queuing

By using the Streams based Advanced Queuing (AQ), user applications can enqueue messages into queues, then propagate them to the subscribing queues. The AQ process sends notifications when messages arrive into queues, allowing the specified action routine to execute. Usually, the action routine involves processing the messages by de-queuing them at the destination.

Oracle AQ has all the standard features of the message queuing systems. It allows the establishment of multi-consumer queues, publish and subscribe methodology, content based routing, transformations, and gateways to other messaging subsystems. Oracle Streams based AQ is fully integrated into the database systems. As a result, the maintenance of persistent queues becomes really robust. AQ stores the messages in the database objects in a transactional order. The messages are available later, even after they are de-queued, for secondary uses like auditing and tracking. This is one of the main reasons for the popularity of AQ.

Event Messaging and Notification

Business organizations need to propagate a variety of messages between different applications running on different systems and supporting a variety of business users. Events are basic units of business communications that convey a certain message, situation, or status, which in turn could trigger a specified action. The alert mechanism or notification mechanism is built upon the simple premise of a cause and effect paradigm.

Streams Methodology event management systems allow the applications to enqueue explicitly. The captured events may be DML or DDL changes. Through the use of multiple queues and queue tables, events are propagated to the desired queue systems. These messages can be explicitly de-queued by writing a suitable application routine. This routine may update certain database objects or trigger some other specific action or series of actions.

Message Systems are important components in the overall business communication process. Based on the appropriate rules, a messaging client or an application can de-queue the messages. This kind of event based system has the added advantage of having the capability of alerting the appropriate monitoring systems or applications groups. They can also develop a suitable auditing mechanism allowing further analysis of the actions that have taken place. User developed application routines can be used to harness the database to perform actions that range from notifying the user that a set criteria has been met or the database can de-queue the messages in a manner determined by the user.

Data Replication with Streams

Data Replication is one of the most widely used methodologies for the maintenance of different sets of data within or outside business organizations. It is used to keep those sets of data synchronized, as required. Data Replication is one of most significant benefits of the Stream Methodology.

Oracle Streams keeps track of database changes and captures those changes in the form of events. These database changes can be DML changes or DDL changes. The changes are wrapped and formatted into Logical Change Records (LCR) and are propagated to the destination system where they are applied to synchronize the database systems.

Streams based replication provides a useful asynchronous replication. This allows the maintenance of remote database systems without affecting performance levels at the source database system. Since the extraction or capture of database changes is effected from the redo log files, it does not delay any transaction activity and does not affect the normal Online Transaction Processing (OLTP) or DSS activity of the source database.

The Oracle Streams methodology provides an effective process for capturing the database changes and then applying them to the data warehousing systems. By using Streams, the capture of redo log information avoids unnecessary overhead on production systems. By using built-in data transformations and user-defined apply procedures, the system has enough flexibility to reformat data or update warehouse-specific data fields as data is loaded. Besides the usual Streams replication technology, Change Data Capture uses some of the components of Streams to identify data that has changed so that the changed data can be loaded into a data warehouse.

The main benefit of the Streams Methodology is the ability to avoid performance overhead. By creating the database changes from the redo log files, near real time data propagation is made possible. Compared to traditional 'select source and load' methods at scheduled intervals, Streams based data loading provides a more controlled and faster refresh of data warehouses. With the built-in, robust rules engine, a variety of data transformations are possible before the data is applied to warehousing systems. Thus, the Streams methodology can be designed in such a way that it can offer many of the standard Extract, Transform and Load (ETL) features for data movement and data loading.

Streams Advanced Replication

Seasoned Oracle Database users and administrators have been using traditional basic and traditional advanced database replication methods for a long time. Both of these systems worked very well, in their own right, for a number of years.

The basic replication system used the store and forward mechanism to transmit the database changes to the destination system. Snapshot based replication was well-suited for the situations in which delays in data refreshes are tolerated. With advanced replication, multi-master replication was possible. By using the 2 phase-commit, real time data replication was possible.

Both of these methods served effectively in most situations, but they caused performance overhead on the source database systems. When database systems were low in both activity and size, the performance degradation was not noticed as much. However, problems were often encountered with large data changes. Plus, configuring, troubleshooting, and resolving conflicts resulted in an increase in administrative overhead.

Oracle Streams, for data replication, is a major feature enhancement that was introduced in Oracle Database Release 9.2. The use of Streams for data replication altered the way in which database changes could be captured, propagated, and applied at the replicated site. This was a big change in replication technology for the Oracle Database system.

Note: Even though Streams supports data replication, it is still possible to configure data replication using traditional advanced replication.

Streams-Based Oracle Advanced Queuing

In Oracle 10g, the Oracle Advanced Queuing system has been integrated with Oracle Streams. The original Oracle Advanced Queuing system has been renamed as Oracle Streams AQ (AQ). The new Streams AQ provides message queuing functionality which is fully integrated into the database system. It is built on top of Oracle Streams and leverages the functions of the Oracle Database so that messages can be stored persistently, propagated between queues on different computers and databases, and transmitted using Oracle Net Services and HTTP(S).

Since the AQ is fully integrated, it has the benefit of high availability, scalability, and reliability that are applicable to the regular database system. Usual database features like recovery, security, and access control are automatically available to the AQ. It is a significant development from the Oracle's commitment point of view. The integration of AQ into Streams and the use of queuing for replication simplify queuing, and each approach compliments the other. This integration is a good step in the direction of providing a comprehensive data management practice. Oracle's future product development efforts will likely be designed to benefit both the Streams and AQ options.

Conclusion

In this chapter, increasing data growth patterns in global business operations have been examined. The need for internal and external data sharing and data movement is ever-growing.

Data replication is an important function of database systems. Oracle Streams provides a new method of data replication and data sharing. The Oracle Streams data sharing methodology is based on the extraction of the database changes from the Oracle Redo Log files. Initially introduced in version 9.2, Oracle Streams is now a fully matured product. The Oracle10g release has brought in many useful features. Some of those new features were highlighted in this chapter as well.

The main points of this chapter include:

- Data accumulation and data synchronization are an important need for many business organizations. It is much more significant for the organizations with multiple sites due to the need to have data exchanged efficiently between sites.

- Data replication conducted by the Oracle Streams replication process helps to achieve data synchronization very effectively by offering time efficient data transfer as well as built-in functionality in the areas of failover and disaster recovery.

- The producer and consumer database model was introduced and was followed by a description of the Oracle Streams methodology.

- Additionally, some third-party products that provide replication and other data sharing capabilities were also examined.

Index

Free!

Oracle 10g Senior DBA Reference Poster

This 24 x 36 inch quick reference includes the important data columns and relationships between the DBA views, allowing you to quickly write complex data dictionary queries.

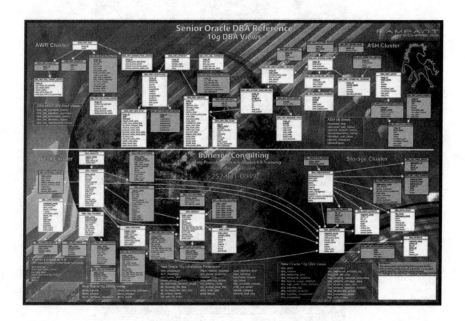

This comprehensive data dictionary reference contains the most important columns from the most important Oracle10g DBA views. Especially useful are the Automated Workload Repository (AWR) and Active Session History (ASH) DBA views.

WARNING - This poster is not suitable for beginners. It is designed for senior Oracle DBAs and requires knowledge of Oracle data dictionary internal structures. You can get your poster at this URL:

www.rampant.cc/poster.htm

Learn Oracle Application Express

Oracle Application Express (formerly called HTML DB) is one of the most exciting web application development tools on the market and this is the first and best HTML-DB Application express book. HTML-DB Application Express is a true Rapid Application Development environment that can take an idea from concept to a working production level application in a very short period of time and this book can help.

This unique book provides easy step-by-step examples to guide you through the various features and removes the guesswork from learning Oracle HTML DB Application Express. Don't be left behind. Learn HTML-DB from the experts!

www.rampant.cc

Oracle Tuning: The Definitive Reference

Oracle 10g has become the most complex database ever created and Oracle tuning has become increasingly complex. This book provides a complete step-by-step approach for holistic Oracle tuning and it is the accumulated knowledge from tuning thousands of Oracle databases.

This is not a book for beginners. Targeted at the senior Oracle DBA, this book dives deep into the internals of the v$ views, the AWR table structures and the new DBA history views. Packed with ready-to-run scripts, you can quickly monitor and identify the most challenging performance issues.

Don't be left behind. Learn Oracle Tuning from the top experts!

www.rampant.cc